International Federation of Library Associations and Institutions

Fédération Internationale des Associations de Bibliothécaires et des Bibliothèques

Internationaler Verband der bibliothekarischen Vereine und Institutionen

Международная Федерация Библиотечных Ассоциаций и Учреждений

Federación Internacional de Asociaciones de Bibliotecarios y Bibliotecas

国际图书馆协会与机构联合会

الاتحاد الدولي لجمعيات ومؤسسات المكتبات

About IFLA   www.ifla.org

IFLA (The International Federation of Library Associations and Institutions) is the leading international body representing the interests of library and information services and their users. It is the global voice of the library and information profession.

IFLA provides information specialists throughout the world with a forum for exchanging ideas and promoting international cooperation, research, and development in all fields of library activity and information service. IFLA is one of the means through which libraries, information centres, and information professionals worldwide can formulate their goals, exert their influence as a group, protect their interests, and find solutions to global problems.

IFLA's aims, objectives, and professional programme can only be fulfilled with the cooperation and active involvement of its members and affiliates. Currently, approximately 1,600 associations, institutions and individuals, from widely divergent cultural back-grounds, are working together to further the goals of the Federation and to promote librarianship on a global level. Through its formal membership, IFLA directly or indirectly represents some 500,000 library and information professionals worldwide.

IFLA pursues its aims through a variety of channels, including the publication of a major journal, as well as guidelines, reports and monographs on a wide range of topics. IFLA organizes workshops and seminars around the world to enhance professional practice and increase awareness of the growing importance of libraries in the digital age. All this is done in collaboration with a number of other non-governmental organizations, funding bodies and international agencies such as UNESCO and WIPO. IFLANET, the Federation's website, is a prime source of information about IFLA, its policies and activities: www.ifla.org

Library and information professionals gather annually at the IFLA World Library and Information Congress, held in August each year in cities around the world.

IFLA was founded in Edinburgh, Scotland, in 1927 at an international conference of national library directors. IFLA was registered in the Netherlands in 1971. The Koninklijke Bibliotheek (Royal Library), the national library of the Netherlands, in The Hague, generously provides the facilities for our headquarters. Regional offices are located in Rio de Janeiro, Brazil; Pretoria, South Africa; and Singapore.

IFLA Publications 146

Digital Library Futures: User Perspectives and Institutional Strategies

Edited by
Ingeborg Verheul, Anna Maria Tammaro and
Steve Witt

De Gruyter Saur

IFLA Publications
edited by Sjoerd Koopman

ISBN 978-3-11-023218-9
e-ISBN 978-3-11-023219-6
ISSN 0344-6891

Bibliographic information published by the Deutsche Nationalibliothek

The Deutsche Nationalbibliothek lists this publication in the Deutsche Nationalbibliografie;
detailed bibliographic data is available in the Internet
at http://dnb.d-nb.de.

Walter de Gruyter GmbH & Co. KG, Berlin, www.degruyter.com

∞ Printed on permanent paper
The paper used in this publication meets the minimum requirements of American National
Standard – Permanence of Paper for Publications and Documents in Libraries and Archives
ANSI/NISO Z39.48-1992 (R1997)

Printing: Strauss GmbH, Mörlenbach

Printed in Germany

TABLE OF CONTENTS

Conference Papers
Inauguration of the Conference

Session 1:
The Digital Library User Experience: a Focus on Current User Research

Session 2:
Digital Library Content: What Users Want and How They Use It

Session 3:

Strategies for Institutions:
Responding to the Digital Challenge

Closing Session

Appendices

ACKNOWLEDGEMENTS

We wish to thank the following organisations for sponsoring the conference:

IFLA Professional Committee
Ministry for Cultural Heritage and Activities (MiBAC) / Central Institute for
the Union Catalogue of Italian Libraries and Bibliographic Information (ICCU),
Italy
The ATHENA Project – Italy
University of Milan / Università Degli Studi di Milano – Italy

Conference Organising Committee

Professional Committee Advisory Board:
Caroline Brazier – British Library, UK
Trine Kolderup Flaten – Bergen Public Library, Norway
Patrice Landry – Swiss National Library, Switzerland
Ingrid Parent – University of British Columbia, Canada
Anna Maria Tammaro – University of Parma, Italy
Ingeborg Verheul – IFLA Headquarters, Netherlands
Steve Witt – Center for Global Studies, University of Illinois, USA

Practical Assistance

Alessandra Stella, Italy
Fabio Venuda, Italy
Dierk Eichel, Germany
Matthias Einbrodt, Italy
Maria Teresa Natale, Italy
Alli Hayes, USA
Chloe Jones, USA

FOREWORD

Increasingly researchers, and also the general public, expect everything to be available on the web immediately, permanently and preferably free of charge at the point of use. Digital libraries create opportunities for cultural heritage institutions to provide wider access to information in a variety of formats through collaboration within the sector (museums, libraries, archives and other memory institutions). Convergence, or cooperation at a cross-cultural level, where libraries, museums and archives work together in creating digital libraries and making their cultural heritage collections available online, is emerging. In many cases digital library projects have lead to successful national collaborative efforts and to a growing extent even to international collaboration initiatives, like the World Digital Library project and the National Libraries Global project. At a European level, Europeana is the project to look at.

In building digital libraries the institutions have to overcome significant barriers. These include the duplication of efforts and overlap in collections; overcoming copyright and intellectual property issues; overcoming matters of quality control; and developing within the profession the management skills to make projects sustainable beyond the initial technical hurdles of development. With the growing focus of libraries on the development of digital collections, the topic is also high on the agenda of IFLA. The numerous institutional perspectives point to several broad areas that the profession needs to address at an international level:

- Training in managing digital library programs and projects;
- Cross-training with cultural institutions to ensure continued opportunities for collaboration and increased interoperability of standards;
- Cross-Domain integration projects / promotion of digital library projects with potential for lateral search engines;
- Broader knowledge within the profession of the way in which libraries and other digital content preservers create the ability to preserve digital content and to ensure the preservation of our future cultural heritage, much of which will be born digital;
- Institutions, in their role of service providers, need to address issues that are affected by Intellectual Property Rights, technical standards, Internet governance, sustainability, economics etcetera.

What is missing? If the user focus is the rightful focus of digital libraries, a broad discussion needs to take place on the political and economic rights of users. What are the implications of moving toward collections of which we may only own access to information, but have no control over the technology that mediates access? Contrary to what we were used to in dealing with paper based content, when it comes to digital content, libraries and even publishers no longer own the technology upon which access to digital information relies.

To promote within IFLA's professional working groups a focus on the user perception of digital libraries, a one day conference was organised in liaison with the general IFLA Congress, on Digital Library Futures, the User Perspective and Institutional Strategies. The IFLA Congress 2009 took place in Milan, Italy. Italy's cultural heritage institutions are heavily involved in cross-cultural digital library projects at an international level. For example with the European projects MINERVA, MICHAEL and ATHENA. At a national level Italy is developing a cross-domain portal with CulturaItalia. Therefore, the Italian Government generously sponsored this event, with co sponsoring of the IFLA Professional Committee. A Professional Committee Advisory Board developed the professional programme; the Italian Government took care of the practical organisation.

The focus of the Digital Library Futures conference was on perceptions and expectations of users for cross domain and multilingual access to museums, libraries and archives digital resources. How can digital library networks be more proactive in promoting user access? If publishers are slowly moving toward e-readers, how can we ensure that these publications are regulated to ensure fair use and access to new forms of cultural productions as well as to what is now considered heritage? The programme gave insight in different strategies for digital libraries and the user perspective, seen from a researcher's or specialist's point of view.

If we want to focus on the user, we need to focus on information behaviour and on interface design, so we were told by Daniel Teruggi and Elke Greifeneder. But what direction is our user taking? In search of information, the user is increasingly consulting the Internet, rather than going to the library. The user now retrieves the information in a different way. David Nicholas from the London University College and Einar Røttingen from the University of Bergen both explored user research behaviour on the Internet. Through the presentations of John Van Oudenaren of the World Digital Library, Rossella Caffo from ICCU, Zhu Qiang from the Beijing University Library and IPA President Herman P. Spruijt it was clear that libraries and cultural institutions are still responding to cultural and technological change. These changes include a proliferation of new media platforms, a rapidly changing intellectual property environment, the development of technical standards, and, of course, financial uncertainty. In his presentation Herman P. Spruijt showed how convergence in the digital area is also present in the dialogue between publishers and librarians, touching upon topics such as digital services, virtual libraries, e-publishing, Google and open access.

At the end of the conference, the IFLA Professional Committee formulated a vision statement that will lead the implementation of the Digital Libraries theme within the IFLA organisation in the coming years. This vision statement is formulated as follows:

"To employ the fullest potential of digital technology in partnership with users by enabling seamless and open access to all types of information without limits to format or geography, and to enhance the ability of libraries, archives and museums to collaborate among themselves and with others to offer the broadest and most complete service possible."

This statement includes the main conclusions: a) technology is not enough; b) we need cooperation with users; c) we need international cooperation with cultural institutions and partnership with others (publishers, et al.).

With this IFLA Publication the IFLA Professional Committee Advisory Board presents the proceedings of this successful conference. In preparation of this publication, the editors wish to thank the authors, who revised their papers, the conference sponsors and the organising committee for making it all happen.

Ingeborg Verheul
Anna Maria Tammaro
Steve Witt   September 2010

CONFERENCE PAPERS

INAUGURATION OF THE CONFERENCE

WELCOME
THE ITALIAN MINISTRY FOR CULTURAL HERITAGE
AND ACTIVITIES AND IFLA

Elio Franzini
Headmaster of the Faculty of Letters
and Philosophy, University of Milan – Milan, Italy

Maurizio Fallace
Director General for Library Heritage, Cultural Institutes and
Copyright, Ministry of Culture, Italy
(Replaced by Rossella Caffo)

Claudia Lux
IFLA President 2007–2009

I would like to open this conference on Digital Library Futures by briefly going back to a tale of the past, that was written on paper and that is narrating a story of paper books. Basically, the tale tells the story of a recluse and his obsession for his library. After dreaming that his books are burned, the man gradually understands that the only safe place for them is his mind.

In 1935, Elias Canetti was very far from the concept of a digital library. However, I feel that most people here, including myself, would find it very easy to understand the deep empathy and caring for books, that is soaking Canetti's tale.

This feeling is our shared ground and our vital link to a long, ancient tradition. It also creates the sense of a continuity where information and culture are processed and circulated through the written word: a circle of culture and knowledge that is never to be broken. In quite recent times, the circle evolved around books and book-like objects that were the basic tools we were used to refer to. Today the circle of culture actually works in the same way, even if its tools are not only paper books, but also electronic objects, *e-mulating* them: books in disguise, so to speak, performing the same cultural task.

So, to conclude, we may agree that the book, in any of its possible disguises, can grant culture the degree of permanence that is needed to turn it into shared tradition. The book is circulated knowledge, and therefore, any strategy to make it more easily accessible, is to make us better human beings.

That is why I'm very happy and pleased to welcome you here, to debate the issues raised by this conference. I would also like to express my deepest gratitude and warm welcome to participants from abroad: any cultural web is to be international, or otherwise it is useless. And any library is to be made into shared knowledge, otherwise it is nothing.

Canetti's huge fictional library may find its place in digital library futures, and be rescued.

(*Elio Franzini*)

First of all, I would like to thank IFLA, in particular IFLA President Claudia Lux and the IFLA Professional Committee Advisory Board for accepting our proposal for this offsite session. I would also like to thank the University of Milano that hosts this conference and cooperated in the organisation. And last, I would also like to thank the ATHENA Project and ICCU, the Central Institute for the Union Catalogue of the Italian Libraries, who supported this initiative.

The Italian Ministry for Cultural Heritage and Activities, and in particular the Director General for Libraries and the Director General for Innovation of the Ministry, is being deeply engaged since many years in national and European initiatives by coordinating digitisation initiatives and promoting access to cultural information and content. All these initiatives are carried on thanks to the cooperation of all the cultural stakeholders at the national and local level and are in line with the ICT plan of the Ministry, the National Plan e-Government 2012 for Italy, and the European Digital Libraries Strategy e2010. We aim to sharing our experiences in cross domain approach to digital libraries, and, generally speaking, to access to the cultural heritage and information with the IFLA international expert audience.

The ICT Strategy of the Ministry is a multi annual programme, focused on the integration of the existing information systems, including those databases which are not aligned with the current standards. The development of a cultural website and portals, the creation of a critical mass of new digital content, all these efforts aim at the quality and the interoperability of the digital content and services. The Ministry promotes this in a cross domain perspective. For instance, the OPAC SBN, the Union catalogue of the Italian libraries, is now integrated and also searchable through CulturaItalia, the Italian Cultural portal. In the same way, MIBAC encouraged the application of interoperability standards among archives, libraries, museums, regions and universities. All the cultural institutions are included: small, large, local, national, public and private. And finally: "Think cross domain", is the sentence that summarizes all the efforts. In conclusion, we hope that with this session, we can contribute to the debate on cross domain digital libraries and to support the start up of an IFLA devoted action line. We wish you a fruitful and successful cooperation at this offsite session of the IFLA Milan international conference.

(*Maurizio Fallace*)

On behalf of the International Federation of Library Associations and Institutions I want to welcome you to the World Library and Information Congress and thank you so much for being here at one of the most interesting sessions, on Digital Library Futures.

About fifteen years ago, when libraries started to discuss and plan how a "Cybrarian", some of you will remember that expression, will work in the future, librarians started to mentally prepare for the Digital Libraries Future. Now, that we still discuss the digital libraries future, it has become much clearer what libraries have to do in a digital world: to organise the world's knowledge, to give access to it. In reality, this is just the same as librarians have done since more than 2000 years. The only small difference is the size of the world we are talking about.

Concerning the users and the material we deal with, a global perspective broadens not only the view of each of us, but introduces complexity and diversity, as much as multilingual aspects. Nevertheless, a global perspective guarantees a wonderful richness of ideas and solutions. And this is where IFLA's conferences and your workshop are all about.

Thank you for joining this session today, and I wish you a lively discussion and great results: usable results for the Future of Digital Libraries.

(Claudia Lux)

INTRODUCTION TO THE CONFERENCE THEME

Patrice Landry

As Chair of the IFLA Professional Committee Advisory Committee that has organised this *Digital Library Futures: User perspectives and Institutional Strategies* conference, it is my pleasure to introduce the sessions and to give our warmest thanks to Professor Elio Franzini of the Università di Milano for welcoming us and for providing this beautiful venue for our conference.

The Professional Committee decided at its December 2008 meeting, that it would support the initiative of the Italian Ministry of Culture to organise this conference, within the framework of the IFLA World Library and Information Congress in Milan in August 2009. An advisory committee was set up to develop a programme that would meet the goals of our Italian colleagues and of the IFLA professional units, the Sections and Special Interests Groups that make up the professional structure of IFLA. Digital collections are now part of libraries' daily work. From managing e-journals to creating born digital documents, from managing digitisation projects to instructing users on copyright issues, or simply creating search accounts for them, library professionals are fully involved in this field.

The tasks of managing and giving access to digital collections are already on the agenda of many of our Sections. The Professional Committee felt that the issue of digitisation should be reinforced with special attention to users' perceptions of digital libraries. In organising this workshop we have made sure that representatives from all of the IFLA sections would be invited, and I am happy to report that most of them are attending this conference.

The Professional Committee also saw the opportunity to further promote the work undertaken by IFLA in the development and promotion of digital libraries. Many of its recent initiatives have come out of the presidential theme of IFLA President Claudia Lux. Her theme, "Libraries on the agenda", has led to the development of several activities in the digital area at a strategic level. The first initiative was to develop a Digital Library Manifesto in order to assist libraries in getting support and funding to set up a digital library.[1] This Manifesto was endorsed in December 2007 by the IFLA Governing Board and is now on UNESCO's agenda. In relation to this work, a working group was set up to develop a set of universal guidelines for digital libraries. They aim to provide a planning and decision making tool for librarians wanting to set up a digital library. A draft version is in progress.

---

[1]   <http://www.ifla.org/en/publications/ifla-manifesto-for-digital-libraries>

The main theme of this conference focuses on the user, as we believe that institutional strategies should take into account the different roles of users in the digital collections. What is the behaviour of users in accessing the digital collections? What do they want and how do they use it? At the same time, this conference will look at how different types of institutions, libraries, museums, archives and publishers are responding to the challenges of providing digital collections that meet the users' needs and interests.

The Advisory Committee did a tremendous job in planning and organising this conference in a very short time, in about six months. This required true dedication from the members of the Advisory Committee and full support of the IFLA Professional Committee and Governing Board. Here I specifically wish to thank the three Chairs of the conference programme, Caroline Brazier, Trine Kolderup Flaten and Ingrid Parent for their work in contacting potential speakers, negotiating the topic of papers and for coordinating the programme. I am also grateful to Anna Maria Tammaro who played a pivotal role in liaising between the Advisory Committee and the Italian sponsors and to Steve Witt for his work in editing the documentation. A special thank you to Ingeborg Verheul, who as IFLA's Communication and Services Director, put all this together. She also was for most of you the main contact in the registration and communication for this conference. The programme reflects their excellent work in making this conference a true success.

I also wish to give special thanks to IFLA President Claudia Lux, and to IFLA President-elect Ellen Tise, for supporting this event and for taking time from their busy schedules for this conference. This is for us a testimony of their support of the digital library issue. I also want to acknowledge the generous financial support provided by Ministry of Culture and ICCU and their role in initiating this conference. And then finally, a special thanks to the speakers for accepting to be part of this conference and to you, the participants, for having accepted our invitation to attend this conference and making it so successful and special.

SESSION 1

THE DIGITAL LIBRARY USER EXPERIENCE:
A FOCUS ON CURRENT USER RESEARCH

THE VIRTUAL SCHOLAR:
THE HARD AND EVIDENTIAL TRUTH

David Nicholas

ABSTRACT

The paper describes and evaluates the information seeking behaviour and usage of scholars in the virtual environment. Data are drawn from a number of CIBER deep log studies conducted over a period of seven years, including studies of users of ScienceDirect, Oxford Scholarship Online and OhioLINK. Hundreds of thousands of scholars, lecturers, researchers and students, from all over the globe are covered in the log analyses. On the basis of these data the characteristics of their "digital footprints" are drawn and evaluated, demonstrating the fascinating and challenging characteristics of the virtual scholar. The paper concludes with a discussion of how information professionals and society at large might best handle a population with a marked preference for fast information and power browsing.

INTRODUCTION

Over the past seven years the CIBER research group[1] at University College London (UK) has been studying the information-seeking behaviour and usage of hundreds of thousands of scholars on a variety of platforms (e.g. Science Direct, MyiLibrary, Oxford Journals, Oxford Scholarship Online, Synergy, British Library Learning Institute) from a wide range of subjects, institutions and countries. This research has resulted in a unique, massive and robust evidence base of how people actually behave on the Web;[2] not how they say or think they behave (the territory inhabited by the ubiquitous questionnaire and most PowerPoint commentators). This is important because "self-report" data are often flawed because people do not remember (or do not want to say) what they do in cyberspace, so we should be wary of what questionnaires in particular tell us. The evidence CIBER have obtained from the server logs of the websites used demands attention as it shows that people are seeking and using information in ways that information professionals have not woken up to or are, perhaps, in denial about. In consequence library and publisher services and systems may well be built on false premises and the wrong paradigms.

---

[1]   <http://www.ucl.ac.uk/infostudies/research/ciber/>
[2]   <http://en.wikipedia.org/wiki/World_Wide_Web>

THE CHANGE AGENTS

Over the past ten years the information landscape and information seeking within it has been transformed by a number of factors, most importantly of all:

1. Massive information choice and unbelievable 24/7, anywhere access to scholarly resources once only the preserve of those fortunate enough to be members of the best universities or national libraries;
2. The digital transition – the fast-forwarding of the user into the digital information environment, a process currently being accelerated by the wide scale appearance of e-scholarly books, which will take huge numbers of students, social science and humanities scholars into the virtual space;
3. Disintermediation, the removal of the intermediary (typically the librarian, but sometimes the publisher) from the information seeking
4. chain, which means we are all librarians now, and have to behave like them – constantly reviewing and validating data;
5. Google provides universal one-stop information retrieval and has made searching simple and very fast; a simplicity and speed which some would argue has encouraged lazy and unthinking searching. The Google search interface is simplicity itself and clearly supports (or leads) to the smash and grab or in and out approach of today's digital information seeker (see later for more on this).

So much change, but what compounds the problem is that the consequences of all this change has gone largely unnoticed, because so much of today's information seeking goes on remotely and anonymously, that information professionals have not fully woken up to this yet. Without this knowledge there is a real danger of working on the basis of an old or false paradigm, which brings with it the inevitable risk of decoupling from the user base – and that is professional death in anyone's language. There is too much looking to the future and too much blaming the kids for a form of behaviour which is endemic to the whole population, which essentially reflects a failure on the part of the profession to deal with what is happening now.

THE CONSEQUENCES OF THESE CHANGES

The digital footprints of the virtual scholar (see the figure below for details of the kinds of data produced) show that: a) there are increasing levels of activity in the scholarly information space and that levels are still rising at an astonishing rate; b) this activity takes place throughout the day, night, weekend and year; c) searching is simple and highly pragmatic; d) in information seeking terms the horizontal has replaced the vertical; e) people power browse rather than read online; f) essentially virtual scholars are navigators; g) there is a great deal of diversity and information seeking and usage varies by discipline, age, gender, type of institution and country of origin; h) user perceptions of brand and authority are not quite what information professionals think.

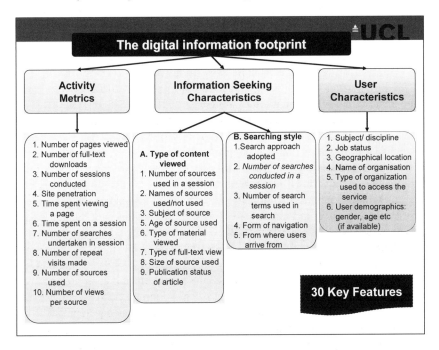

Digital information footprint of the virtual scholar – from the server logs

TREMENDOUS ACTIVITY GOING UP ENORMOUSLY

Access is the main driver with many more people being drawn into the scholarly information net. We are all scholars, now that scholarly information is so freely available. Everyone is now connected to the big fat information pipe, courtesy of broadband, to which only specialised and privileged institutions once were. Also, existing scholars can now search much more freely and flexibly from the office, home, the café, airport and train, and all that raises the volume of their use. There are just so many more opportunities to search now. Above all, the logs tell us that scholarly information is hugely popular, and we (publishers and librarians) should all rejoice in this.

Despite being ten years into the digital scholarly revolution, levels of current growth are astonishing with recent annual growth rates, exceeding 50% in the case of some publisher databases. This is because of:

- Improved access via wireless connection, making home use attractive;
- Increasing population of students worldwide;
- Increased digitisation of back titles, making scholarly resources attractive;
- Increasing impact of e-journal Big Deals;
- The preference of the young to have everything digital – maybe not even aware there is a hard copy alternative;
- Increasing use of Course Management Systems, like Blackboard and WebCT, by teaching staff including online reading lists with easy links to journal articles and course text books and therefore students can access material with minimum effort.

Yes, lots of activity, but much of this constitutes "noise", which unfortunately is too readily mistaken for demand and satisfaction by database owners and web managers. Thus, the majority of users of many sites are robots, spiders and intelligent agents that are responsible for organising the digital environment, disseminating data and providing access to material. In the case of The House of Commons Intranet in the UK around 90% of all usage was accounted for by robots and the percentage is increasing! This, more than anything else, demonstrates that we are witnessing a fundamental change in the information environment – robots, even scholarly ones, are a wholly new user phenomenon. As we shall learn, even in regard to genuine human activity, much of it is of a light and passing nature.

Use is also very volatile, varying dramatically according to month, day of the week and hour of the day. This can be put down to the fact; a) that enormous bodies of users are moved around the virtual space, in very quick time, by search engines that constantly refresh the information landscape, offering new choices; b) new and competing products and services are continually coming online.

SCHOLARS SEARCH AND USE ALL THE TIME

Logs are fantastic for discovering exactly when scholars search for and use information. What they show is that 24/7 anywhere access is delivering a good deal of scholarly productivity with academics using services well into the night and over the weekend. Thus a recent CIBER study[3] showed that a quarter of ScienceDirect use occurs outside the "traditional" working (9-5) day and weekends account for around 15% of use (delivering another working day!). Some things never change, however, and lunch time is still the busiest time

---

[3]   <http://www.rin.ac.uk/our-work/communicating-and-disseminating-research/e-journals-their-use-value-and-impact>

and Monday lunch time is the busiest of all; interestingly, this is also true for e-shoppers.[4] E-book use is quite different to e-journal use and is very much more tied to the rhythms of the teaching terms and closely related to the modules being taken.

SHOLARS LIKE IT SIMPLE

Much to the displeasure of librarians, users avoid carefully-crafted discovery systems and opt for simplicity and convenience every time. Some examples to illustrate this:

- advanced searching, offered by virtually every scholarly database, is used rarely and hardly at all by users in highly-rated research institutions, the people who you might expect would use it. Indeed, anecdote would have it that only librarians use the advanced facility;
- scholarly website add-ons and innovations, like email alerts, virtual learning environments and blogs, are distinctly a minority sport;
- Google searching is attractive to scholars of all kinds and of all levels.

Thus just 4 months after ScienceDirect journals[5] was opened to Google indexing a third of traffic to physics journals arrived via Google. This is particularly notable since physics is richly endowed with well established and innovative information systems and services. Another example: Historians on Oxford Journals[6] proved to be the biggest users of Google. Forget stereotypes, historians could hardly be further away from the stereotypical Google user. While Google searching is hugely popular, once users enter a site, they browse rather than search via the internal search engine; they did not trust it to deliver.

THE HORIZONTAL HAS REPLACED THE VERTICAL

The logs show that scholars are promiscuous in information terms; around 40% of visitors do not come back regularly, if at all. What they also do, and this is partly a function of promiscuity, is "bounce" or flick across the panoramic information terrain, viewing just 1- 3 pages at each site they visit, much to the consternation of web managers who hope that users will make the most of the hundreds of pages on offer. We can put this form of behaviour down to four main factors:

---

[4] David Nicholas and Ian Rowlands (2007). Digital Consumers. London; Facet
[5] <http://www.sciencedirect.com/>
[6] <http://www.oxfordjournals.org/>

- Huge and increasing choice means they shop around, lured here and there by the ubiquitous search engine;
- Basic retrieval skills – the average user enters 2.3 words in their query and constructs no more than two iterations of a search – means that they often turn up irrelevant links. There is a huge attrition rate and a general acceptance of search failure on the part of users. This can be largely explained by a shortage of time and avoidance of information overload. The fact that many leave their memories behind them in cyberspace adds to the "churn" or promiscuity rate;
- A direct result of end-users checking relevance for themselves;
- Age – the younger they are, the more bouncing they do and more promiscuous they are. And gender: men are more promiscuous than women.

It would be a mistake to assume that bouncing necessarily represents "failure at the terminal" because sometimes it represents a highly direct and pragmatic form of information seeking. Users enter a site knowing exactly what they want, not wanting to waste any time, having done their homework elsewhere so as to avoid the pitfalls of searches which lead to information overload. What we are witnessing is the opposite of airline fast-bag drop: fast-bag pick-up!

VIEWING HAS REPLACED READING

The big question of course is whether viewing has replaced reading. There is certainly very little evidence of scholars reading online. When they look at a full text article it is generally for a period of less than five minutes. Shorter articles are preferred to long ones, and if they are long, they are more likely to read the abstract only. This is not surprising in a world in which scholars have been conditioned by emailing, text messaging and PowerPoint. There is a sense that scholars go online to avoid reading.

Of course scholars might be downloading and reading offline at a more convenient time and in a more preferable format (paper) – a form of behaviour we call "squirreling". While a good number of downloads are read at a later date there can be no doubt that many are not read and instead scholars hope that through a form of "digital osmosis" the content will eventually enter their brains via the mouse.

What has replaced reading is "power browsing". Hoovering through sites, titles, content pages and abstracts at a huge rate of knots has it benefits and pleasures as on interviewee told us:

> "I can update my knowledge very quickly…the sheer number of books is overwhelming, if I can look at them very quickly – you know within 15 minutes, I can look at 3 or 4 books – and get some very superficial knowledge of what is in

them, nevertheless it improves my scholarship, because in the back of my mind, these books already exist."

Scholars have become navigators, people who love to travel but do not always like getting there. Navigating towards content in very large digital spaces is of course a major activity. People spend half their time viewing content, the rest of the time they are trying to find their way to it or avoiding it.

DIVERSITY RULES

While there is a lot in common between scholars in regards to how they seek and use information there are also big differences. Scholars are a diverse group and the great thing about log analysis is that you are working with huge populations and thus can drill down to discover diversity. The main areas of significant diversity found follow with examples:

- Subject studied: Life Scientists are absolutely insatiable when it comes to scholarly information and typically account for nearly half of all e-journal use – admittedly they are a large community with a very large scholarly resource.
- Scholars from research-intensive universities behave very differently to those from teaching orientated universities. Thus research intensive universities use per capita is highest, their users spend much less time on visit, and they forsake most of the online facilities and make most use of gateway sites, like PubMed.
- Searching: Germans are the most "successful" searchers and most active information seekers if we take into account the number of searches obtaining positive outcomes and highest number of pages viewed in a session.
- Age: older users are more likely to come back (they are less promiscuous), and view abstracts. Young people use Google more and spend more time online viewing.

BRAND: MORE COMPLICATED THAN YOU THINK

There are two important aspects to this topic. Firstly, it is extremely difficult in cyberspace to determine whose information it actually is. This is because there are so many players involved. Take the example of a search of ScienceDirect conducted from the office of an academic. They power up their *Toshiba* laptop, connect it to *UCL*'s network via an Ethernet cable. They then fire up their *Firefox* browser to connect to the Web. They put in *ScienceDirect* into the *Google* search box. They enter the site and note that *Elsevier* are responsible for ScienceDirect. They then browse the list of journals and choose *Acta Mathematica Scientia*, which they notice is the journal of the *Wuhan Institute of Physics and Mathematics*. They alight on an article by *Emam Tarek* from the *Department of Mathematics, Faculty of Science, Suez Canal University, Suez, Egypt*. See the problem: there are ten possible names to choose from.

Secondly, even if it is possible to establish whose information it is, there is another issue: whether it is thought to have come from a good or bad brand? This is far from straightforward. Take the following case. During a CIBER study a touch screen health kiosk was placed near the pharmacy in a well know European supermarket, Tesco. The owner of the kiosk was SurgeryDoor, a health information company and the information on the kiosk was produced by the British Government's National Health Service (NHS). When supermarket customers, who used it, were asked whose information they thought it was, a majority said: Tesco. When told by the interviewer that is was actually NHS information, many were disappointed and the younger they were, the more disappointed they were. Tesco is a very successful company selling all kinds of things in addition to food, like insurances. It is a trusted brand for many. On the other hand the NHS is regularly criticised in the British media for its failure to look after its patients. This is worrying, perhaps.

CONCLUSIONS

In broad terms then the scholar's information seeking and usage behaviour can be portrayed as being frenetic, pragmatic, bouncing, navigating, checking and viewing. It is also promiscuous, diverse and volatile. Now these are not terms you are going to find in the established text books of our profession. Yet it is by no means certain than "bouncing" and "power browsing" are a wholly new phenomenon. The virtual environment allows us to view information usage and seeking and the resulting outcomes in detail and on an unbelievable scale because every action of everyone who uses a site is recorded. However, this was not the case in the physical information environment and in reality we really knew very little about how people behaved and, in the information vacuum, when someone, for instance, took out a book or bought a paper, the assumption was that they read it all. So maybe we were living a lie and now we know the reality – we have always been bouncers; the universe of linear exposition, quiet contemplation, disciplined reading and study was just an ideal which we all (librarians especially) bought into and (more worryingly, perhaps) developed information services and products around accordingly. The difference is, of course, (and this is where the concerns really should lie) that the opportunities for bouncing are now legion and this has created ever more bouncing and the pace is not letting-up. It is whether this is all leading to major changes in the way we obtain knowledge, particularly whether this constitutes a possible "dumbing down",[7] that concerns us most. What is certain though, is that we (young and old; the naïve and those that know better) have taken to fast information as we have to fast food. In the words of an *Observer* journalist:

> "What Marshall McLuhan called 'the Gutenberg galaxy' – that universe of linear exposition, quiet contemplation, disciplined reading and study – is imploding, and we don't know if what will replace it will be better or worse. But at least you can find the Wikipedia entry for 'Gutenberg galaxy' in 0.34 seconds."[8]

As a society and profession we are going to have to face up to the consequences and a good start would be to wake up to what has actually happened to our users. Only then can we determine for ourselves the consequences that result from what is absent from increasing numbers of our customers – a lack of a mental map, no sense of collection, and a poor idea of what is good and relevant. Understanding information seeking behaviour in the digital space is a prerequisite to determining academic outcomes – positive and negative. Then we shall be in a position to determine whether we are really benefiting from the information society and always on information, and if not, whose responsibility it is?

---

[7] <http://en.wikipedia.org/wiki/Dumbing_down>

[8] Naughton, J. (2008), Thanks, Gutenberg – But We're too Pressed for Time to Read, at: <http:// www.guardian.co.uk/media/2008/jan/27/internet.pressandpublishing>

WHO ARE THE USERS OF DIGITAL LIBRARIES? WHAT DO THEY EXPECT AND WANT? THE EUROPEANA EXPERIENCE

Daniel Teruggi

ABSTRACT

The ambition of *Europeana* is to make European cultural content accessible through its portal, providing a unique access point where any kind of media is represented. It is oriented towards the general public but also to professionals and scholars. The user perspective is then essential for the success and acceptation of the project. How can this feedback be obtained; do users expect something specific? Are they really looking for something or just wandering around? Independently from traditional statistic and survey actions, it is important to obtain the perception users have of Europeana and to thus structure and orient a portal that represents a new way of accessing culture.

WHAT IS A USER?

Within the web domain, users are considered as the main recipients for services and websites. Their feedback and input is extremely important to analyse the success of an offer and in many cases to justify the investment and the efforts made to capture them as well as the potential revenue that can be generated. Users can be classified in representative categories, however it is important to keep in mind that the same user may belong to different categories and have different behaviours in function of the profile under which he is using the website:

- General users: people that use a system seeking some kind of result, just for curiosity, for need or for entertainment;
- Specialised users: people that get highly acquainted with a specific tool or website, without being a professional user;
- Professional users: people that use tools or websites highly relying on them in order to get specific results;
- Representative users: people that "know something" and are used for defining user-requirements, testing and specifying needs.

Many of today's more popular social websites are based on implementing open services, with no content inside. The users introduce their content and establish the links with other users, thus creating a community or social environment. When websites propose content, for cultural or financial reasons, they have to be very attractive and contain important volumes in order to generate use of the content and eventually generate an associated network.

Europeana is a cultural portal for accessing European content.[1] When launching the prototype portal in November 2008, it was important to get feedback regarding the way users were dealing with the portal, the use they were making of it, as well as the difficulties or frustrations they could encounter during their exploration. Several methods were then applied in order to understand users and in order to improve the capacities and interaction of the portal and prepare new versions of it.

DEVELOPING A PORTAL SERVICE

When conceiving a tool, software or website there is a certain number of usability considerations with which designers and developers work. They concern the nature of the users, their identified or hypothetical needs or wants, in which context they will be using the services and what their background as users is.

Before even trying to answer these interrogations, there is a general analysis on what usability is and how it relates to the conception of the service. In general *usability* is defined as the ease with which people can grasp the sense and employ a tool or object in order to achieve a particular goal. Usability is highly depending on *Human-computer interaction*, which represents the elegance and clarity with which the interaction with a program or website is designed. In order to be user-friendly, the interactions have to be *Efficient, Easy and Satisfying*.

Certain specific constraints exist on the web; websites have to be grasped immediately. Users just land on websites and they have to understand the way to move around and the potentialities of the environment. There is nothing like a manual to learn how to use a website, there is no time for learning or for tutorials. This leads to a certain number of concepts that may measure the usability of a website; these concepts permit us to classify and analyse websites in order to judge their efficiency. Among them we find: *Learnability, Efficiency, Navigation friendly, Memorability, Common errors*. The overall objective is to provide *Satisfaction* to users, in relation with the content and services of the website or portal.

---

[1] <http://www.europeana.eu>

USER REQUIREMENTS

The objectives and ambitions of a website, portal or service are defined by the user requirements, which define the set of needs, necessary for any project to be successful. They define what a system should do and how; they are previous to any development. Three types or requirements are identified:

- **Functional requirements**: what do you want a system to do; for example: *"I want a vehicle capable of transporting material from one place to the other"*. Functional requirements define the overall objective of the system;
- **Non-functional requirements**: restrictions on the types of solutions that will meet the functional requirements *"It has to be capable of transporting 2 tons of material, not larger than 1m80 or higher than 2m"*. Non-functional requirements define the constraints that will condition the way the system will be developed;
- **Design objectives**: are the guides to use in selecting a solution *"Easy to use, red seats, plastic doors..."* User friendly or; simple to access, are ways of defining how users will apprehend the system.

REQUIREMENTS IN EUROPEANA

When developing the Europeana prototype, it was important to clearly identify the requirements, while checking them with the different actors involved in the project: the design and development team, content holders and potential users. The requirements were thus expressed as follows:

- **Functional requirements: a** multilingual portal to access European cultural content from 4 domains: Libraries, Archives, Audiovisual Collections and Museums;
- **Non-functional requirements**: the portal should be capable of containing up to 10 million objects, permit multiple access, not contain the content but metadata, previews and representations permitting access to content in their original environments, respect publishing and author rights;
- **Design objectives**: should be user friendly and permit different categories of users to make the best out of it. It should contain a certain number of user-oriented functionalities (*My Europeana, Send to a friend, Communities*, etc).

Once the requirements were decided and the technological choices were made, it was important to identify the profile of the potential users of the portal. Some users were clearly identified through existing local experiences on online content. Other users had to be modelled and discussions had to be undertaken to verify their eventual expectations based on the description of what the portal would be.

 – **General user**: people that visit the Europeana portal just for curiosity or seeking sporadically for a specific information or content;
 – **School child, Student**: permits to conceive online courses or to prepare presentations and exercises; it is one of the great potentials for Europeana, it makes access to cultural content easy;
 – **Academic student, Teacher**: looking for certified information, and the possibility of exporting information for courses or research works;
 – **Expert researcher:** explores all the possible sources, annotates and uses them thoroughly, wants access to the largest possible amount of content;
 – **Professional user**: experts in the domain, archivists, librarians, curators, searching and verifying information and creating links among content;
 – **Content holders**: they know what they have and how to access it; they need to check their online access.

Several workshops with representatives of the domains were organised to discuss and evaluate the general user functionalities that would be implemented on the portal. These requirements and the profiles were very important in the development of the first prototype of Europeana, launched in November 2008. The event was highly publicised and it generated a strong user attraction, which completely overloaded the portal to the point it had to be closed down for 3 weeks. Once the first spike in use ceased, it was important to start applying user satisfaction measuring tools in order to understand how users were dealing with the portal, identify usability problems, and collect user expectations. The information gathered during this process would then be used in the conception and requirements of the further versions of Europeana and would help decision-making as well as defining the specifications needed in order to attain users' expectations. It would also provide information about the success of the portal and the evolution of its use through time, thus providing statistics of how it is accessed and the number of consulted documents.

MEASURING USER SATISFACTION

There are different approaches to get user feedback; none of them is exclusive so it is important to work with all of them and combine their results:

 – **On-line surveys:** questionnaires answered voluntarily by users;
 – **Feedback inbox**: reactions that users spontaneously send through emails;
 – **Login analysis**: analysing connections, to obtain statistic information;

- **Focus groups surveys**: observing groups of users in action;
- **User testing panel**: selected panel of users testing new versions;
- **Expert analysis**: expert analysis evaluation of usability and interface.

ON-LINE SURVEYS

On-line surveys were the first action taken and began in May 2009. Users had to answer an online questionnaire which would give answers to specific questions concerning the portal and its usability:

- Frequency of use of Europeana;
- Use and ratings of features and functions;
- Stages reached in a search;
- Use of *My Europeana;*
- Interest in additional services;
- Likely future use of Europeana.

3200 results were collected, which is quite a high level of response. An i-pod was offered as a prize to one of the contributors randomly selected. The more interesting comments found in the survey were:

- A large amount of users did not see "My Europeana" or didn't understand what it was about;
- Users want to publish their own content in the portal;
- Users would want chat possibilities (young users).

The survey was important also to identify the age of the users; there were few answers from users under 20, and a peak around 45 to 65 years of age. It also permitted to identify the professions of users. Many categories were present but more than a third didn't specify any specific profession. Users came from 9 European countries, with a majority from France.

FEEDBACK INBOX

Feedback inbox reactions were sent by users who voluntarily expressed their opinion either to congratulate, to propose new technical facilities, to request for new partners, or to simply ask questions (or criticize). The Europeana office answers most of the questions and organises the results in different categories. From February 2009 to July 2009 nearly one thousand messages were received in the different categories:

Categories	Percentage (number of emails received)
Congratulatory	22% (203)
Technical (including: registration, languages, spelling, bugs, API's, search issues etc.)	18% (170)
Unknown Languages	11% (99)
Partner Requests	10% (92)
Content	9% (87)
Content Strategy Requests	5% (42)
Suggestions	5% (50)
Companies	4% (35)
Press List	4% (39)
Abusive	4% (39)
Student questions	1% (6)
Job requests	1% (9)

LOGIN ANALYSIS

Login analysis is based on software that parses log files from a web server. Based on the values contained in the log file, indicators are derived on who, when, and how a web server is visited. Reports are generated from the log files immediately, but the log files can alternatively be parsed to a database and reports generated on demand. An external company was identified to realise the analysis and the compilation of results in order to get a regular feedback about access to the portal and the origins and types of navigation that is realised by users.

FOCUS GROUPS SURVEYS

The first focus groups surveys will be started in November 2009. Four different groups from different countries will be studied while they are using Europeana. The principle is to select a specific group in terms of age or geographic location. Once the group is identified, several sessions are organised where users freely navigate on the portal, while an expert observes their movements and reactions. Thus a clearer view on how users move around the portal and which difficulties they may encounter is obtained.

USER TESTING PANEL

Based on the results of the online survey, a group of 17 people, representing different countries, ages and professions, was selected. The selected persons were asked officially if they would be interested in testing the new versions of Europeana and to participate in evaluations. The group will meet for the first time in March 2010 in Paris for a presentation of the specifications of the next version of Europeana, due to be launched during the summer. Regular meetings will be held every six months with the group.

EXPERT ANALYSIS

Expert analysis is to be undertaken in September 2009 by two experts named by Ina (Institute nationale de l'audiovisuel) in France in order to analyse from a scientific approach the functioning of the site and its coherence with the major user trends on websites. The conclusions were very positive, with several indispensible behaviours:

- The access to information is always under 3 clicks;
- The front page gathers all the important information to navigate;
- The front page permits one to directly activate the principle function and access secondary content (News, My Europeana); The design permits easy identification;
- The links are useful and clear.

The site establishes high credibility, but new users cannot, from the information on the front page, immediately realise the size and richness of collections featured in the site.

Some incoherencies were identified mainly concerning the use of different languages while navigating. The desired result is usually not found with just one search, but with more refined searches. Better filtering could also be developed in order to simplify the access to information.

CONCLUSIONS

Measuring user satisfaction is a permanent objective for Europeana; this is a continuously evolving project, where new content is regularly introduced and indexed and new versions are developed. At the same time, usability expectations change regularly with new interaction developments arriving on the web, new social paradigms and new ways of accessing and exchanging information. Europeana has to get a clear feedback on what users like or think, on how the portal fulfils their expectations from a content point of view. At the same time the project has to follow user tendencies and adapt the environment to new expectations.

One of the important questions is how to let users interact on a higher level with the portal. They have expressed their interest in contributing content for

Europeana, however the main characteristic of Europeana's content is that it is certified through the institutions that contribute to it. User contributions are indeed potentially rich and would contribute to enlarge the content or to create complementary views on it. These issues are being evaluated and solutions could be possible where the certified environment is preserved, yet user contributions enrich institutional contributions. This is the next step for Europeana as it strives to improve in response to needs and suggestions.

A CONTENT ANALYSIS ON THE USE OF METHODS IN ONLINE USER RESEARCH

Elke Greifeneder

ABSTRACT

This paper will build on the Digital Library Federation-sponsored study by Denise Troll Covey (2002, *Usage and usability assessment: library practices and concerns*) to look at the state of the art of user research. One of the questions is whether the data that comes from people's research actually answers their research question. This is especially important for digital content because the methods that we often apply come from a non-digital world. An example of such a problem is asking only people physically in a library about a resource that is available worldwide.

INTRODUCTION

Purposeful data results from an expressed purpose in combination with an adequate method. Data gathering is an essential part of online user studies, and every method has its areas of application and its limitations: quantitative surveys are limited in their ability to detect causal relations; with qualitative interviews broad generalizations are risky. In library and information science, user research is a domain in which we gather large amounts of data. But is our data really "purposeful"? Already in 1972, Frank Heidtmann made the criticism that we use inadequate research techniques and that these research techniques are – independent of their appropriateness – used in an inaccurate and invalid way.[1]

In 2002, Denise Troll Covey[2] interviewed participants from the Digital Library Federation (DLF) about their use of and experience with methods in user research. She stated that "Libraries are struggling to find the right measures on which to base their decisions. DLF respondents expressed concern that data are being gathered for historical reasons or because they are easy to gather, rather than because they serve useful, articulated purposes". All studies are "assessing

---

[1] Heidtmann, Frank (1972). Zur Theorie und Praxis der Benutzerforschung: Unter besonderer Berücksichtigung der Informationsbenutzer von Universitätsbibliotheken. München-Pullach: Verl. Dokumentation. (p. 36-37).

[2] Troll Covey, Denise (2002). Usage and Usability Assessment: Library Practices and Concerns. Washington, DC: Council on Library and Information Resources, At: <http://www.diglib.org/publs/dlf096/dlf096.htm> (p. 2-3; 7-8; 24 and 35).

use and usability of online collections and services"– they all deal with online user research. Online user research means our studies focus on an (online) digital library environment. Hence, our users are online. What does this mean for our research? Digital library users are no longer tied to a local place. Online users of digital libraries are multi-local, multi-lingual and live in multiple time-zones. Getting "purposeful data" in online user research requires that the research be done online because the users are there.

RELATED WORK

Most of the research on users and digital libraries analyses a single digital library and its users. The content analysis illustrates this with a sample list of 70 publications.[3] The number of publications on specific methods is limited. Edgar (2006), Homewood (2003), Xia (2003), and Nicholson (forthcoming 2010) discuss general research design issues.[4] Studies like "The virtual scholar: the hard and evidential truth" try to draw a general picture of online users.[5] The described content analysis grows out of Troll Covey's study (2002) that addresses the relation of purposes and methods in online user research. She concluded that "Libraries are struggling to find the right measures on which to base their decisions" (p. 2).

RESEARCH PROBLEM

Not all methods are currently usable online; focus groups are difficult in an online environment, as are interviews and ethnographic observations. Surveys or log file analyses are on the other hand more easily used for online studies. All the studies Troll Covey analyzed in her research were about an online environment, but she did not ask whether the study itself happens online or offline. Another limitation of her study is her population: 24 relatively rich libraries that can afford staff time and money for intensive user research. This paper

---

[3] Greifeneder, Elke (2009) Sample Online User Research in LIS, Available at: <http://www.elke.greifeneder.de/UserResearch>

[4] Edgar, Bill (2006). Questioning LibQUAL+: Critiquing its Assessment of Academic Library Effectiveness. In: *Proceedings of the ASIS&T Annual Meeting*. At <http:www.asis.org/Conferences/AM06/papers.112.html>; Homewood, Janet; Huntington, Paul and Nicholas, David (2003). Assessing used content across five digital health information services using transaction log files. *Journal of Information Science* 29 (6); Xia, Wei (2003). Digital library services: perceptions and expectations of user communities and librarians in a New Zealand academic library. Australian Academic and Research Libraries 34 (1), 56-70. At: <http://www.alia.org.au/publishing/aarl/34.1/full.text/xia.html>

[5] Nicholas, David (2010). See the article in this publication.

addresses both limitations. With the analysis of international publications on digital user research during the last ten years it has a broader scope and it considers whether the method was used on- or offline. The content analysis also examined the stated purposes in online user research and the relationship between that purpose and the result. Due to space considerations, the results of this analysis of purposes will be separately published.

RESEARCH DESIGN

The method used to answer these questions is a content analysis using thematic coding. Within the analysis, six categories haven been used:

1) Method;
2) Purpose;
3) Result;
4) Offline/online;
5) Object of study;
6) Type of researcher.

In an additional step, each category was divided into several subcategories. For example the main category "methods" splits into subcategories including surveys, focus groups and log file analyses. In this research, "in-vivo" codes have been used that derive directly from the data. For example an author writes "the purpose of this study is to measure the use of our electronic services with a survey". Thus the purpose is "use", the object is "electronic services" and the method is a "survey". A second step encodes these original statements into abstract groups for further analysis. Most qualitative data analysis programs require the full documents to be imported, but this was not possible with these publications. Therefore the analysis was done by hand in Microsoft Excel. Below is an illustrative example of four of the publications that were analysed. The examples show the content analysis process, including the original in-vivo codes, a first coding (that summarized several different descriptions to the code "use"), and finally an enhanced numeric encoding for computer-based measurement.

Document type	Thesis	Thesis	Conference Paper	Journal paper
Year	2007	2001	2004	2001
Title	Online virtual chat library reference service: A quantitative and qualitative analysis	Le risorse elettroniche di un sistema bibliotecario: analisi e monitoraggio del loro utilizzo	Website entries from a web log file perspective: a new log file measure	Evaluación de la base de datos ISOC a través de un estudio de usuarios : Homenaje a José María Sánchez Nistal
Method	12 content analysis	2 log file analysis	2 log file analysis	1 survey
Details about method	analysis of reference transcripts; builds on other studies and guidelines	log file analysis and online questionnaire and costs analysis	Web Entry Factor (WEF)	paper and email questionnaire sent to users and to reference librarians, open and closed questions
Researcher type	1 student	1 student	1 student	2 LIS school faculty
Purpose of study	7 to provide a theoretical conceptual model of best practices for the reference interview	2 + 3 find out how users use the system AND analyze use-cost-relation AND satisfaction measurement	2 use + user patterns	2+ 3 + 9 information about the use + satisfaction measurement + measurement of quality
Relation purpose and result	5 purpose does not match result; it is a method of measurement	3 purpose match result, – but very static analysis of use	3 purpose matches result, but log file analysis of webpage, no user behavior or patterns but more general usage frequencies	2+ 3 + 6 purpose matches result, but use is only defined as how often someone clicks on something and satisfaction is measured in asking directly how satisfied someone is with something
Object of study	7 reference service	2 electronic resources	1 institutional web page	23 internal electronic resources
Offline/ online	0 offline	1 online	1 online	0 offline

Table 1: Illustrative example of the analysis of four publications

If a study used two methods, for example an interview and a survey, it counted both as a survey and an interview. As a result, the total of all methods is higher than the number of publications. This approach considers the fact that some methods are applied in combination in order to collect separate kinds of data, for example the study by John Crawford used focus groups, a survey and a citation analysis in order to "monitor off-campus usage of EIS [electronic information services], the use of pass worded databases, and the freely available internet" (p. 1). 11 % of all publications (8 of the 70 studies) make use of a combination of methods: mainly surveys, interviews and usability-tests are combined.[6]

The aim of this content analysis is to identify methods we use in online user research. The analysis is based on the following sampling criteria:

The five article databases are DABI, E-LIS, DissOnline, ProQuest and LISA. DissOnline, the German thesis repository, and ProQuest Dissertation Abstract, the international database for US/Canadian thesis, cover the current research on a high scholarly level. LISA, Library and Information Science Abstracts, is the international database for the LIS field and serves as a supplier for peer-reviewed articles. E-Lis, E-Prints in Library and Information Science (LIS), is an Open-Access Repository and covers for this analysis the part of current user research mainly within conference proceedings and serves as a European counter balance to the mainly US research in LISA and ProQuest. Finally, DABI is a German journal database that contains only abstracts of articles that have been published in the German community. These articles are mainly non peer-reviewed. They are used in this analysis to include the current user research in smaller (and poorer) institutions.

The publications that have been taken into consideration contain applied user research in a digital library environment and examine only online services. The sampling excluded the opening hours of the local institution, satisfaction with local staff, and general observations about human behavior. All publications post-date 1998.[7] The sample contains no unpublished conference contributions and no slides from conference presentations. For the retrieval process, the databases classifications were used. In DABI these were the keywords "Benutzerforschung", "Studie", "Umfrage", "Befragung" and "Fragebogen",[8] in E-LIS the subject terms "use studies" and "user studies", within LISA the descriptor combinations "[use AND Digital Libraries]", as well as "[studies AND Digital Libraries]", "[survey AND Digital Libraries]" and "[focus groups]. DissOnline offers no classification within LIS, nor does ProQuest, so the search query "[all thesis within LIS AND 1998–2009] served as basis for sorting in subject to the sampling criteria.

---

[6]   Crawford, John (2003). The use of electronic information services by students at Glasgow Caledonian University: background to the project and introductory focus groups. *Library and Information Research* 27, no. 86, p. 30-36, At: <http://eprints.rclis.org/3413>

[7]   In 1999, the DSL technology is introduced in Germany and in 2000 the typical Swiss man spent 12.5 minutes a day online. The broad use of digital collections started only after 1998.

[8]   Translation: user research, study, poll, questionnaire, survey.

The content analysis included a total of 13 thesis, 13 conference papers and 44 articles, of which 52 % are peer-reviewed articles, 34 % are non-peer-reviewed articles from DABI (that means in German and research from smaller institutions) and 14 % are non-peer-reviewed articles from E-LIS.

RESEARCH LIMITATIONS

Of course, these 70 publications are not the whole research that is done in online user research in LIS. Much of user research is done without publishing the results, because user studies are often conducted in order to make concrete improvements in a system or in a service, rather than with any intention to publish the results as research. There are no exact numbers how big this grey zone is. A member of the German National Library reported in a discussion that they have averaged one user research study per year since 2000 – but only two were published and can be found using the criteria above. In this example the ration of published to unpublished studies is about 1 to 4 or 25%. The 70 publications in this study offer only a picture, showing tendencies in methods and purposes. It may be reasonable to guess that only the best and most interesting projects result in a publication. If that is true, then the analysis paints a picture of user research in LIS that shows only its best parts.

RESULTS OF THE ANALYSIS: METHODS USED

Most of the online user research is done by students (36 % of all studies). That is not a surprising number, since user research is a popular subject for bachelor, master and doctoral theses. The other groups are librarians working in libraries, who do 31 % of all studies, and LIS school faculty and staff, who do 26% of all studies. In 7 % of the cases, an external non-LIS-professional conducted or helped with the study. As mentioned earlier, one study might have several people from different groups working on it. Each group counted one. It is striking that in those studies where the result matched the purpose, an external expert person was generally involved.

The most frequently studied of online user research has been electronic resources with 33 %. Such electronic resources are often licensed and not accessible without appropriate authentication. In critical financial times, libraries need to prove the value of these electronic resources. Free digital libraries are the second mostly studied object with 22 %. Only 9% of the studies cover the local OPAC.

Based on the data, libraries use fewer surveys[9] and a greater variety of methods than may be obvious. Nonetheless 43 % of all user-research methods are

---

[9]   Surveys in this analysis mean a questionnaire with a (mostly highly) structured form. Surveys do not include open-ended interviews.

still surveys. Remember that a study using both a survey and a focus group, counts both for the survey and for the focus group categories. This means that in nearly half of all the studies, researchers used a survey. Log file analysis follows in popularity with 18 %, followed by interview with 12 % (see the graphic below). An additional interesting fact is that surveys are used by all kind of researcher groups, but that students favor log file analysis.

Troll Covey offers different results in her study, but there too surveys are used by most of the researchers. While "most of the DLF respondents" (p. 35) used log files in her study, not even one-fifths does it in the current analysis. Even more obvious are the differences in qualitative methods such as focus groups: "more than half of the DLF respondents" (p. 17) use them contrast to a use of 4 % in the current analysis. One possible reason for these differences may be that DLF members have more money to spend for qualitative research and for a multiple-methods approach than others have. It could also be that people said in the interviews that they did a focus group that was really only a meeting with student assistants. The reason for the differences could also be found in the published data. Perhaps people actually did interviews at the beginning of their research, but did not mention them in the final publication. In any case the numbers in this analysis are not what people have said they did in an interview, but what they took seriously enough to publish under their own name.

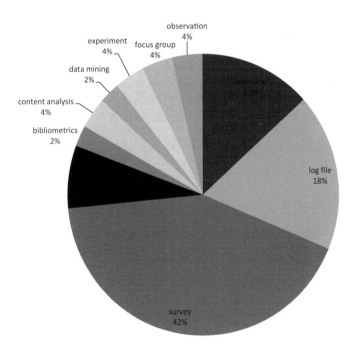

Graphic 1: Methods used for online user research

OFFLINE OR ONLINE

The initial question for this content analysis was where the research has taken place. The analysis shows that still nearly 50 % of the online user research is held offline (for example, in focus groups in local libraries). The highest online rates come from the university faculty and staff in Library and Information Science. See the following graphic.

	offline	online
student	48 %	52 %
librarian	45 %	55 %
university faculty and staff members in LIS	39 %	61 %

Table 2: Online User Research – offline or online?

A second important question is: which methods are specifically used online? The content analysis reveals that the only method that is used predominantly online is log file analysis – a method where no human interaction is necessary during the data collection process. Similar reasons hold for online-surveys, which also rely only on machine-based interactions. The high number of off-line surveys in the graphic 3 may be an outgrowth of the state of user research at the beginning of the analysis period, due to the domination of the survey method at this time. The first email survey dates back to 1999, the earliest online survey in the publication set took place in 2001. The first think-aloud test (in the publication set) happened only in 2002, and the first interview was done in 2003. Methods like interviews or focus groups currently take place nearly entirely offline. Only one of the studies used an online interview. Only in 21% of the cases did researchers use a qualitative method (focus groups, interviews or observations) – more than double that number used surveys.

	log file	survey	interview	focus group
offline	20 %	66 %	91 %	100 %
online	80 %	34 %	9 %	

Table 3: Methods used offline and online

Qualitative methods traditionally require human-to-human communication between the interviewer and the interviewee to be able to reformulate a question or to respond to a specific answer in order to get deeper insights into behavior. An example of qualitative research in usability engineering comes from the construction of persona and scenarios for a digital library – for both, deep insight into sample users is needed, rather than data about the whole population. Quantitative methods may be used afterwards to check if the persona or the scenario matches the population. Despite artificial intelligence experiments, machines currently cannot effectively conduct unstructured interviews on their own.

The problem is that quantitative research designs require knowledge about the user's context to be able to ask the right questions and to interpret the data in the right way. Do closed answer-sets offer the options that users would provide or do they only the questioner's perspective? Can log files be analysed without knowing the full social context of the users' actions? If most people select new offerings, does this mean that they want that particular information or are they merely browsing? The analysis above shows that surveys are used for many more purposes than all the other methods and that they are often used as an all-purpose research tool for need assessments, user typologies, perception studies, satisfaction testing – even for testing usability.

CONCLUSIONS

Although researchers may use quantitative methods, they tend to articulate purposes like user typologies or need assessments that implicitly demand qualitative methods with an interactive human presence. If the purpose is to know users and the context in which they use a digital library, human-mediated inquiries need to substitute for surveys and log file analysis. As Notess says: "Part of the problem is that the log files do not tell us anything about user motivation or rationale. For instance, we noted that only 11% of user sessions used bookmarking. But we do not know why the other 89% did not make use of this feature."[10]

In several of the studies that were considered, the authors themselves commented that they better need qualitative data for their own purposes or that they gathered within a survey qualitative data but did not know how to interpret the results. For example Lehnard-Bruch (2005) used some open-ended questions in her survey and had to admit that "the analysis of the open-ended questions like 'what can the library do to improve its service?' and 'what are additional offers you would like to see in your library?' proved to be difficult, because the answers are very heterogeneous and because many answers are only mentioned once"[11] (p.147). Sarah Diepolder (2003) obviously had problems in analyzing her data and had to refer to interpretations that were pure speculation: "The high number of identified changes in the search strategy may be a result of [...] it also might be a result of [...]"[12] (p. 29). Jina Choi Wakimoto (2006) used a

---

[10] Notess, Mark (2004). Three looks at users: a comparison of methods for studying digital library use. *Information Research* 9, no. 3. At: <http://informationr.net/ir/9-3/paper177.html>.

[11] Lehnard-Bruch, Susanne, Barbara Koelges and Ute Bahrs. (2005). Benutzerumfrage der Landesbibliotheken im Landesbibliothekszentrum. *Bibliotheken heute* 1 (3), p.147-48. Original citation: Die Auswertung der offenen Fragen *Was könnte die Landesbibliothek an ihrem Serviceangebot verbessern?* und *Welche weiteren Angebote würden Sie sich wünschen?* gestaltete sich als schwierig, da die Antworten sehr heterogen sind und es viele Einzelnennungen gibt.

[12] Diepolder, Sarah (2003). Was ist eine Körperschaft?: Umfrage zur Opac-Nutzung an der Universitätsbibliothek Tübingen. *BUB* 55, no. 1, p. 28-30. Original citation: Die hohe Zahl der dabei

mostly closed-ended survey and adds in his publication: "Perhaps most telling were the comments received from 38 percent of survey respondents"[13] (p. 129).

It is necessary to add that researchers using qualitative methods also had problems: Don MacMillan (2007) used a focus group and said that "We found the analysis and reporting stage more time-consuming and difficult than expected. This stage requires advance planning and use of qualitative analysis methodology."[14] (p. 430). The problem is not only the need to use qualitative methods but to know how to use them. More research about online qualitative methods and more training is necessary.

Further References:

Alcaín, Mª Dolores, Piedad Baranda, Luis Rodríguez Yunta, Adelaida Román, and Ángel Villagrá. (2001). Evaluación de la base de datos ISOC a través de un estudio de usuarios: Homenaje a José María Sánchez Nistal. *Revista Española de Documentación Científica* 24, no. 3. p. 275–88, At: <http://eprints.rclis.org/9741>.

Harmeyer, Dave (2007). Online virtual chat library reference service: A quantitative and qualitative analysis. Pepperdine University, California.

Mayr, Philipp (2004). Website entries from a web log file perspective: a new log file measure. In AoIR-ASIST 2004 Workshop on Web Science Research Methods, Brighton, At: <http://eprints.rclis.org/2831> .

Nicholson, Scott (2005). A framework for Internet archeology: Discovering use patterns in digital library and Web–based information resources. First Monday 10 (2). At: <http://firstmonday.org>.

Riolo, Massimo (2001). Le risorse elettroniche di un sistema bibliotecario: analisi e monitoraggio del loro utilizzo. Diploma Universitario thesis, Università degli Studi di Milano Bicocca (Italy). At: <http://eprints.rclis.org/2793>.

---

ermittelten Strategieänderungen (70 Prozent) kann möglicherweise daraus resultieren, dass [...] es könnte aber auch […].

[13] Wakimoto, Jina Choi, David S. Walker, and Katherine S. Dabbour (2006). The myths and realities of SFX in academic libraries. *Journal of Academic Librarianship* 32, no. 2.

[14] MacMillan, Don, Susan McKee, and Shawna Sadler. (2007). Getting everyone on the same page: a staff focus group study for library web site redesign. *Reference Services Review* 35, no. 3, p. 425-433.

SESSION 2

DIGITAL LIBRARY CONTENT:
WHAT USERS WANT AND HOW THEY USE IT

A PIANIST'S USE OF THE DIGITISED VERSION
OF THE EDVARD GRIEG COLLECTION

Einar Røttingen

ABSTRACT

This paper gives a user-perspective on the digitised version of the Edvard Grieg Collection in Norway. In recent years, an increasing number of collections and archives of music-related material has become available on the Internet. Through this instant access to our musical heritage, performers, researchers and music lovers all over the world can gain information and knowledge about a composer's work and live. As a performing artist, researcher and music teacher, the author provides examples from his own work with Grieg's music and the Edvard Grieg Collection and gives some perspectives concerning how this recent development is of importance to the many users in his field.

PROFESSIONAL BACKGROUND

First of all, let me say a few words about my professional background. I work as a professional pianist as well as a Professor of Music Performance at the Grieg Academy at the University of Bergen in Norway. This involves teaching piano, chamber music and supervising the Masters Program in Music Performance and Composition. In my work I combine the roles of being a performing artist, researcher and teacher and it is in these connections I will talk about my work as a user of the digitised version of *The Grieg Collection.*[1]

DIGITAL MUSIC COLLECTIONS AND ARCHIVES

It is safe to say that there has been an amazing activity during the last 15 years or so concerning the digitisation of music collections and archives. The Grieg Collection is only one of many that are now digitised and available on the Internet. Let me briefly mention a few of these projects. A well-known example is the Neue Mozart Ausgabe, mainly operated by the Internationale Stiftung Mozarteum in Salzburg.[2] It includes the musical texts and critical commentaries of the entire Neue Mozart-Ausgabe published by Bärenreiter Verlag in

---

[1] <http://www.bergen.folkebibl.no/grieg-samlingen/engelsk/grieg_intro_eng.html>
[2] <http://dme.mozarteum.at>

Germany. The comprehensive project *Digital Beethoven House* was initiated in 1996, and includes handwritten music, letters, first editions, sculptures and musical instruments as well as utensils gathered in the course of over 110 years.[3] Recent on-going projects include *Bach Digital*, a collaboration started in the year 2000 between the Bach-Archive in Leipzig, the Staatsbibliothek zu Berlin and the Sächsiche Landesbibliotek in Dresden.[4] This includes autograph manuscripts and other sources primarily displayed for research purposes. There is also the *Schubert online* project, considered to be the largest collection on the net with over 500 autograph scores, letters and documents related to Schubert's life. The collection is based on documents of the Wienbibliothek im Rathaus, but also includes documents of other institutions in order to become even more comprehensive and aims to collect all the existing material into one singular website and network system.[5]

There are, of course, other examples of digitised archives, but these are some of the most well known, presenting famous classical composers that are in great demand and often performed worldwide.

THE GRIEG COLLECTION

In 1906, 10 months before his death, Grieg added a codicil to his will. In this will he and his wife, Nina, wanted to give his music manuscripts, articles and letters, printed music, books and other material to The Bergen Public Library at the condition that it would be preserved for aftertime. They wanted the collection to be easily accessible to the general public. In 1919 Troldhaugen, their residence in Bergen was sold at a public auction, and the documents, letters and scores were handed over to the library. In 1930 Nina Grieg, from her home in Denmark, sent her unique collection of letters from musicians, artists, authors, etc. Over the years the collection of original documents has expanded through gifts and purchases. The Grieg-archives are continuously updated with all new literature, recordings, documents and other information on Grieg and his music.

In 1989 a proposal was made for a pilot project for the digitisation of the material in The Grieg Collection. The Library initiated the considerable undertaking of transferring the archive to digital forms, thereby preserving the original documents while at the same time contributing to greater accessibility. The digitisation process itself started in 1990, and thus became the pioneering reference-project for the subsequent digitisation of other archives and collections in the years to come. A pilot-project was shown during the Grieg jubilee-year

---

[3]   <http://www.beethoven-haus-bonn.de>
[4]   <http://www.bach-digital.de>
[5]   <http://www.schubert-online.at>

of 1993. Ten years later, in 2003, the complete 25.000 pages of documents were finally available on the net and open to the general public. The presentation system was excellently done, the handwriting had been transcribed, metadata was added and supplementary information such as articles etc. was in place – all of this giving music researchers and music lovers the opportunity of finding their own way around in this comprehensive collection – very much in the spirit of Edvard Grieg's own wish of public "accessibility". The Grieg Collection web pages have today about 300.000-400.000 visits per page per year, coming from more than 30.000 different PCs.

COLLABORATION AND JOINT EFFORTS

Two points should be made before proceeding here. The digitisation and presentation of these kinds of collections on the net would not have been as successful as it was without close collaboration between the different people involved. This includes close contact between the music researchers, librarians, designers and computer and networking experts. These groups often have different skills and different backgrounds, but in addition they do not necessarily understand each other from the beginning, often having different ideas and using different terminology and methods of working. In this process, it is of special importance that researchers help to edit and prepare the different material for the online presentations. For The Grieg Collection this cooperation functioned very well from the beginning, owing to the fact that several of the experts had already considerable experience from the job of critically editing Grieg's complete works in the 1980s. The second point to be made is the importance of joining forces in a joint collaboration between different institutions for the common purpose of collecting all material into one singular online system and network. In this way, as in the Schubert online project I mentioned earlier, all available material can be found in one place, creating better accessibility for the user.

THE IMPORTANCE OF GRIEG ON THE NET

Why is it important to have access to Grieg's autograph manuscripts on the net? For me, as a performer within the European art of music tradition, the musical score is the starting point for my work within an orally transmitted tradition. For centuries performers have interpreted scores since the early days of musical notation in the medieval era.

Today, we have access to an incredible amount of notated music – spanning over 600 years – that is brought to life every time it is performed or recorded. The composer's autograph manuscript is most often the starting point for published editions and therefore a prime source of reference for publishers and musicians. In our age of interest in historical performance practice, autograph manuscripts can be essential in gaining knowledge on matters of importance for the performer.

DIGGING DEEPER INTO THE COLLECTION

I will now give an example of what we can find in an autograph manuscript that is to be found on the on-line version of The Grieg Collection. I want to present some of my own studies of one of Edvard Grieg's most important piano pieces: *Ballade – in the form of variations on a Norwegian folk tune op.24*, composed in 1876. This piece was part of my PhD-project on three Norwegian piano works by Grieg, Geirr Tveitt and Fartein Valen, and was finished in 2006.

BALLADE OP. 24

Edvard Grieg's *Ballade op. 24* has been and remains a controversial and myth-enshrouded work. The *Ballade's* coming into existence is known to be closely connected to critical circumstances during a particular phase of the composer's life. "Written in heart-blood in days filled with sorrow and despair", Grieg wrote, many years later, of the *Ballade's* genesis. In the autumn of 1875, both Grieg's father and mother died. In Grieg's letters from that time, we can follow his process from depression and artistic hiatus to the gradual emergence of the *Ballade* through the winter of 1875–1876 in Bergen. There seems to be a close relationship between the work and Grieg's own grieving-process, as well as a wish to get on with life. Later, Grieg referred to this period as an important turning point for him. Gradually, he found renewed faith in himself and in life.

Let's take a look at the autograph manuscript and find out what kind of information can be of use for a performing musician. This concerns both matters of practical value and aspects related to the composer's own work-process that can contribute to a greater understanding of the *Ballade*'s coming-in-to-being.

Let's look at the first of the three existing pages. First of all we can see that Grieg initially wanted to call the piece *Capriccio* – which implies a much shorter work, consisting of the theme and a couple of variations. We can see that he has tried to scribble over the original title and instead write *Ballade – in the form of variations over a Norwegian folk tune*. This shows the composer's process of deciding on a title for the piece, and then changing his mind. Originally Grieg had obviously not thought of the piece as the large scale composition it finally would be. The *Ballade* eventually turned in to a piece of approximately 20 minutes, containing 14 variations on the theme.

The autograph is incomplete and only has 3 of the 14 variations. These 3 variations are also in a different order than the later version. This proves that Grieg initially thought of a different progression of variations, probably connected to the more modest concept of a Capriccio. One of the variations in the autograph manuscript, the 4th, is not used in the final version of the *Ballade*. It shows that Grieg obviously was trying to explore the theme's possibilities, developing more variations than he needed for the final version. But when the idea of a continuous narrative eventually evolved, this particular variation did not fit in with the "story". The final order seems definite and this superfluous variation obviously cannot be included without destroying the structure of the piece. In for example Robert Schumann's *Symphonic Etudes op.13*, the additional etudes or variations that where initially extracted from the piece by the composer, are often included in modern performances. Contrary to Grieg's *Ballade*, the structure of Schumann's etudes gives room for an open and flexible form.

Of special interest is the theme itself. We can see that he has changed the melodic tones of the original version, which was written down and harmonized by Ludwig M. Lindeman, a folk music collector in Norway. Grieg had Lindeman's version as a point of departure and then removed the dance-like features by slowing down the tempo from Moderato to Andante – to a more elegiac and singing character – and re-harmonizing the melody with the use of chromaticism.

Of interest is also the change of character-implications for the performer. We can read from the autograph manuscript that Grieg has started out by writing Andante serioso (serious) and Andante doloroso (painful), but ended up with Andante espressivo (expressive). My theory is that Grieg thought of serioso and doloroso as too loaded with personal emotion so that the term espressivo, indicating a general expressivity, was preferred, inspiring the performer, as it does, to a broader range of expressive imagination, without restraining the character to personal sadness and melancholy. The richness of feeling is particularly evident in Grieg's harmonic coloring. The melancholy of the Ballade has many shades, which include moments of light and hope.

Let's look at how a detailed performing instruction in the autograph manuscript has brought controversy in aftertime. If we look at the autograph, we can find an indication of diminuendo in the theme. It is written twice as a small hairpin. In the printed editions from Grieg's lifetime, this hair-pin is omitted. It seems that Grieg deliberately omitted it in the approved printed versions. In the new *Henle*-edition of the *Ballade* from the 1980s, this hair-pin has surprisingly reappeared. The editors have reinstated it from the autograph and chosen to interpret it as an indication that was initially a good instruction for musical purposes. They prefer Grieg's initial idea even though Grieg omitted it in the printed version. Has Grieg overlooked this hair-pin in the autograph when he approved the first editions? Was he conscious of the removal of it? The fact remains; we will probably never know the answer to these questions. However, this example shows that editing musical scores is always an act of interpretation of the sources. This case shows how important it is to have access to the autograph in order to see what Grieg originally wrote in order to make your own choices.

THE ADVANTAGE OF THE DIGITISED

It would be possible to do a full-text search and find comments in Grieg's correspondences, diaries or articles that could be of significance for understanding the *Ballade* and the interpretation of it. One can, for example find Grieg's own critique of live performances of the *Ballade* that he attended, played by famous performers, and read correspondences with his editor Edition Peters in Leipzig, with comments that confirm Grieg's doubts about the piece, his initial idea of a *Capriccio* and his gradual process in regaining confidence in his own artistic abilities. Letters and correspondences can be important sources for the performer's studies of musical works.

As we have seen in this example, having instant access to Grieg's autograph manuscript of the *Ballade* is an invaluable source of information for anybody who wants to study and play this piece, whether you are a pianist in Germany, Brazil, Japan, Kenya or Australia or anywhere else where there is access to the internet. You don't need to travel to The Bergen Public Library in Norway.

DIGITAL COLLECTIONS AND TEACHING

I now want to give you an example of the need for access to autograph manuscripts from my own teaching experience. All my performing master students at the Grieg Academy have to do an in-depth project during their 2-year studies. They explore a field of interest such as a particular piece of music that they are playing, a composer, performance practice issues, a style or instrumental method. In my daily work as a supervisor for these students, there is often a need for obtaining sources such as autograph scores. I was supervisor for a guitar student who was studying the guitar-sonata of the important Spanish composer Turina. He had to go to Madrid personally in order to have access to the autograph score and other sources on Turina – and to make a copy of the autograph – which is not always possible because of copyright laws. He found out many interesting deviances from the printed edition which had been edited by the notorious Segovia, who often changed the scores considerably to suite his particular performance purposes. If the Turina manuscripts were obtainable on the net, my student would not have had to travel to Madrid.

Of course, sometimes you have to personally see the score or other documents, as in musicological research. You can then see the ink, paper quality and other specific details. But for ordinary use, it is usually sufficient to see the scores and other documents on the net.

172 SONGS FOR VOICE AND PIANO

I want to say a few words about a current on-going project that I am involved in. The project concerns Edvard Grieg's 172 songs for voice and piano. My colleague, the Norwegian bass-baritone Njål Sparbo, has written all the songs on to his computer on the Finale score-writing software. This enormous under-taking has been done for the reason that most of the songs only exist for the so-prano or high voice register. In order for Mr. Sparbo to sing these songs, he must transcribe the scores to a lower register and key. Because of this special computer program, he can print out every song in any desirable key within a few seconds. I am now helping him look through the piano part and proof-reading it. In the process we also need access to *The Grieg Collection's* auto-graph manuscripts on the net in order to double-check with the current com-plete Peters-edition. We will also be working with a linguist who will provide phonetic symbols for all the songs so that any foreign, non-Scandinavian singer can perform the songs with Norwegian texts. All of this will in the near future be available on the net so that any singer can download any song by Grieg in any key, with information on the texts and authors, translation of the texts and an attempt at interpreting it (to tell what the song is about) and with interna-tional phonetic symbols that anybody can read in order to get the right Norwe-gian pronunciation. So far, you can today already go in and order the songs in any key at this website. At a low cost, you can download the transposed song to your computer.

This is a unique project that will make Grieg's songs much more accessible and practical for singers all over the world. Grieg's songs, which form a large part of his total output and are some of his most important compositions, have until know been little known beyond the Nordic countries. In my opinion, they should be considered among the great songs of the romantic era alongside those of Schubert, Schumann and Brahms. Thanks to the Internet, all obstacles of making this music available and ready for use up till now will be gone. This is a good example of what a digitised, on-line collection as The Grieg Collec-tion can inspire performers to do. In this case it has contributed to furthering the idea of reaching out to a greater number of interested users of all kind in order to keep an important song tradition alive by laying the groundwork for future performances.

CONCLUSIONS

I believe that the access to scores and archives on the net is important for the future interest in the classical music tradition. It will strengthen the music's possibility to reach out and sustain its position in our culture with the possibil-ity of gaining greater interest in the composers, their music and scores. As a user, it has been inspiring to see the recent development in digitisation. I am sure that this is something that Grieg and his colleagues in their wildest fantasies did not dream of could happen! The development is truly sensational, something we tend to forget, as we as human beings quickly become accustomed to taking any new revolutionary technological development for granted.

The expertise and knowledge that has been obtained so far in this digitisation-development should be shared among the people involved, so that the best possible presentation of the material can be accomplished. For future projects, it is important that the owners of documents collaborate in making joint systems that collect the relevant material into carefully prepared presentations on the net that are made in a way that users can easily find what they are searching for and also easily can connect to related information. The users have an important function in the processes involved because they know what is needed for practical purposes. The key word is collaboration, not just between the individual people involved, like researchers and experts on the relevant material, but also between institutions, such as libraries, archives, publishers, governmental ministries, foundations and other public and private sponsors.

Our motivation for collaborating should simply be that we all have a common interest in making this cultural heritage obtainable and alive for the present and future generations. In the seemingly cultural chaos of today's world, we need this attitude of "preserving for the future" more than ever.

WHEN IS A LIBRARY NOT A LIBRARY?

Susan Hazan

ABSTRACT

When the Library of Congress uploads 4,880 of its 14 million pictures to Flickr, UNESCO tries to fit the Memory of the World into a global library in order to guard it against collective amnesia, and the New Bibliotheca Alexandrina becomes the home of the Wayback Machine, the mammoth Internet Archive that contains a snapshot of all web pages on every website since 1996, you know that it is time to rethink the term "library" in a way that makes sense for the 21st Century. This paper discusses one of the more resounding clashes that are currently taking place around the world when the traditional librarian meets the Web 2.0 library head on.

INTRODUCTION

We usually know what is in store for us when we visit cultural institutions online. Through our familiarity with the physical institution – the library, archive and museum – we are fully confident that when we encounter their counterpoints online we will discover a real "smorgasbord" of rich digital holdings – a feast for our eyes and our souls. We can pick and choose from many different kinds of online content; confident in the quality and integrity of the collections and exhibitions that stems from the knowledge that we are aware that they have been authored, and published, by the institutions themselves.

This is the Internet that we have grown familiar with; a world wide library where organisations and institutions publish their content, through the broadcast model of producer (institutions, organisations or individuals who produce content) to consumer (in this case the end user). The broadcast model is a reminiscent of the way we use our televisions – zapping from one channel to the next with our remote controls from the comfort of the armchair – only, when we search for content online, we tend to sit up straight and let the mouse and keyboard propel us through our pathways. Even though we travel the breadth of World Wide Web virtually unhindered, this is an experience that is understood to be a passive one. As we click our way searching, saving, printing, and sending to others, we still do so very much in consumer mode; with few opportunities to respond, modify, or contribute to what we discover.

As the web has become more participatory, there are now more and more opportunities for individuals – in addition to the traditional producers – to make their voices heard and to actively create, manage and publish their own micro-content. Thus the traditional consumer profile has evolved into the notion of the "prosumer" a term first coined by Alvin Toffler[1] in his 1980 book, *The Third Wave*, to describe the blurring of the role of producer and consumer. Prosumers act over Web 2.0 platforms, and take on new roles which no longer fall into distinct categories of producer and consumer. Together with the popularity of peer-to-peer communications on social networks, this could be seen as a direct assault on those who traditionally act as the gatekeepers of knowledge (such as memory institutions) who, before the development of Web 2.0, had mostly applied a traditional, broadcast model approach and were confident that it was they who held the exclusive mandate to manage cultural content.

Much has been written about the participatory nature of Web 2.0, as it has gradually evolved since the early 2000's. During this period, many innovative projects emerged from cultural institutions – even before the term Web 2.0 was coined.[2] The appearance of what we now call Web 2.0 brought with it the growth of blogs, wikis, and wiki-like tools that enable end users to not only read other's content, but to generate and publish their own micro-data. Rather than simply describing a new set of standards or services, the social tools and the authoring interfaces that now characterise Web 2.0, in fact, signify a paradigm shift in the ways we use the Internet. The emerging model can now be understood as a multi-channel model, where the web acts as a conduit, running through distributed networks that make connections not only between cultural institutions and their users, but also from individual to individual. Clearly users still want quality content that is one click away but the question is – where are they going to look for it?

Most studies now agree that users[3] and particularly online, native, (young) users, are spending more time on social networks rather than the silos of Internet 1.0.[4] If cultural institutions do not seamlessly interface into these spaces, their content will simply not be delivered to users in those sites where today's users are at home, and profusely active. According to Nielsen,[5] Facebook not only actively reaches to 54.28% of users but the popular social network site engages them for much longer on the site than other sites do.

---

[1] Toffler, Alvin (1980). The third wave, New York Morow.

[2] Susan Hazan, Weaving Community Webs: A Position Paper, DigiCULT Thematic Issue 5: Virtual Communities and Collaboration. At: <http://www.digicult.info/downloads/digicult_ thematicissue5 _ january_2004.pdf.>

[3] The share of adult internet users who have a profile on an online social network site has more than quadrupled in the past four years – from 8% in 2005 to 35% now, according to the Pew Internet & American Life Project's December 2008 tracking survey <http://www.pewinternet.org/ Reports/2009/Adults-and-Social-Network-Websites.aspx>

[4] Overall, around 49 percent of Internet users are also using social network sites, <http:// www.readwriteweb.com/archives/twitter_use_up_among_internet_social_network_mobil.php>

[5] <http://en-us.nielsen.com/rankings/insights/rankings/internet>

RANK	PARENT	UNIQUE AUDIENCE (000)	ACTIVE REACH %	TIME PER PERSON (HH:MM:SS)
1	GOOGLE	153,928	79.24	2:36:52
2	MICROSOFT	136,639	70.34	2:08:38
3	YAHOO!	134,688	69.33	3:08:28
4	FACEBOOK	105,449	54.28	5:24:38

Table 1: Top 10 U.S. Web Parent Companies, Home & Work, September '09

This has serious implications for traditional cultural institutions and with the explosion of so much community-based activity taking place on Web 2.0 interfaces, it is time to examine the role of the cultural institution in an information society, and more explicitly, the changing face of the institutions' web presences as they represent the institution online.

THE ONLINE DIGITAL LIBRARY

At a time where the barely two-decades-old Internet is growing at breakneck speed, the physical institutions inevitably evolve at a slower rate and are straining to meet the challenges the digital library presents. While the physical library has made impressive strides in making their collections available electronically, has established standards that are implemented worldwide, and is developing services that extend beyond their physical walls, they are now bracing for developments that change the very concept of the printed book: the e-book and the growing range of on-demand e-publications. Your local library maybe the place you remember visiting in your childhood; carting a string bag home once a week bursting with the weekend's reading. You may recall the school library; fondly evoking memories as the place you were to first discovered all your favourite authors and illustrators. The imposing university library might be the place where you spent hours, pouring over piles of books preparing for exams and assignments, but when you simply need to gesture to your mobile phone, book reader or PDA, anywhere or anytime to call up your favorite book, we have to pause and consider what is happening to all those places we once called *our* library?

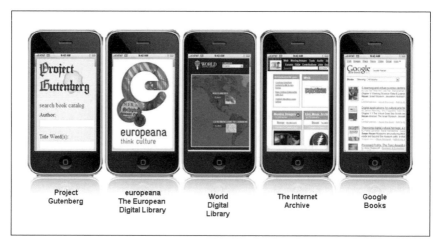

Graphic 1: Digital libraries at your fingertips

Out of the hundreds, possibly thousands of digital libraries now online,[6] this paper provides a brief overview of a selection of the exceptional digital libraries now open to the prosumer: *Project Gutenberg*[7] the first of the major libraries to appear online, *Europeana*, Europe's Digital Library; UNESCO's ambitious *World Digital Library*; the *Internet Archive* as the home of the *Wayback Machine*[8] and *Google Books*.[9] At the same time libraries are taking on leading roles and are also making impressive inroads into the electronic arena, responding to these new challenges as they reach out to their public beyond their traditional mandate. This paper will discuss the *Library of Congress* which, in addition to opening up impressive content on its own institutional website has uploaded over 7,000 of its 14 million photographs from its collection to the popular photo-sharing network at Flickr.[10] As a specific case study, this paper will showcase some of the impressive services that the Nebraska State Library offers over Web 2.0 platform to highlight one of the more resounding clashes of civilisations that are currently taking place around the world when the traditional librarian meets the Web 2.0 library head on.

---

[6] See for example: List of digital library projects from Wikipedia <http://en.wikipedia.org/wiki/List_of_digital_library_projects>
[7] Project Gutenberg <http://www.gutenberg.org>
[8] The Wayback Machine at the Internet Archive, <http://web.archive.org>
[9] Google Books, <http://books.google.com/books>
[10] Library of congress Photographs on Flickr <http://www.flickr.com/photos/Library_of_Congress>

PROJECT GUTENBERG

Founded in 1971 by Michael S. Hart, with a mission to encourage the creation and distribution of eBooks, the Gutenberg Project has the distinction of being the oldest of the digital libraries. According to their website most of the items in their collection are the full texts of public domain books, and currently (December 2009), Project Gutenberg claim 30,000 items in their collection. With a self-defined mandate to digitise, archive and distribute cultural works Project Gutenberg has made a wealth of classic literature openly available to the public in ASCII versions.

E-Books can be downloaded to the PC, mobile device, or other portable reading device. As the individual pages are scanned and turned into editable text by OCR processing (optical character recognition), the Project Gutenberg staff call on other volunteers in the internet-based community to proofread the scanned texts; a practice they call distributed proofreading. In terms of copyright issues, the US-based Gutenberg Project argues that they offer only publications in the public domain. This is pertinent in the US only, and users outside of the US are required to abide by their own national copyright laws. There are currently some 50 other languages represented with each numbering up to 50 books in the collection. In addition there are sets in a range of languages with more than 50 books in the collection in: Chinese, Dutch, English, Esperanto, Finnish, French, German, Italian, Latin, Portuguese, Spanish, Swedish, Tagalog (an Ustronesian language spoken in the Philippines by about 22 million people).[11] With this substantial bank of e-publications already one click away, Michael S. Hart has already made an inspiring contribution to making classical literature available, and accessible to anyone who may wish to read at his or her leisure anyplace and at anytime.

EUROPEANA: EUROPE'S DIGITAL LIBRARY

While Michael S. Hart's vision was intrinsically in English, the library public in Europe is concerned not only that their library be accessible in all the European languages, but even more critical, that their content should be fully embedded in Europe's cultural identity; reflected not only in language but also as an expression of the cultural heritage of each country and of each ethnic community. Europeana,[12] Europe's, multimedia, digital library grants access to the cultural holdings of Europe's twenty seven member states. Europeana includes books, maps, recordings, photographs, archival documents, paintings and films from national libraries, museums and galleries, archives, libraries, audio-visual

[11] Talgalog language see <http://en.wikipedia.org/wiki/Tagalog_language>
[12] See the article of Daniel Teruggi in this publication.

collections, and cultural institutions.[13] The goal of Europeana is to open up new ways of exploring Europe's heritage through free access to Europe's greatest collections and masterpieces integrated into a web portal available in all of the EU languages.

Overseen by the EDL Foundation,[14] Europeana draws in Europe's rich heritage; combining multicultural and multilingual environments, and introducing innovative technological solutions, standards, and new business models. Europeana's current prototype will reach full service in July 2010 with full functionality in the Rhine Release, with a proposed 10 million digital objects. The second phase of the project, the Danube Release, will see the launch in 2011 of a fully-operational Europeana.eu with improved multilingualism, and semantic web features.

While the management section and the technical information on the website are maintained solely in English, being the working language of Europeana, the top level pages, i.e.: "navigation", "search", "retrieval" and "display" interfaces are available in all the partner languages: Bulgarian, Catalonian, Czech, Danish, Dutch, English, Estonian, Finnish, French, German, Greek, Hungarian, Icelandic, Irish, Italian, Latvian, Lithuanian, Maltese, Norwegian, Polish, Portuguese, Romanian, Slovakian, Slovenian, Spanish, and Swedish. A search in one of the languages of the European library links to objects that then can be then viewed in their original context. A typical search, such as on *Hamlet*, will result in 34 texts, 465 images, 18 videos and 12 sounds. Users can then choose from the translations available; such as the Hungarian translation; HAMLET, Dán királyfi, Willian Shakespeare, Fordította: Arany János[15] that opens in a new window. This kind of multilingual access allows each member of the European community to be able to search in their own language and discover resources, fully embedded in their original cultural heritage. Individual institutions that have contributed their content into Europeana are clearly identified; granting national, professional, and cultural distinctiveness of the content that makes up the supra-European identity, drawing in all cultures and all nationalities into the coherent whole.

This highly ambitious project covers a very broad range of cultural heritage including:

- Text: books, letters, archival papers, dissertations, poems, newspapers, articles, facsimiles, manuscripts and music scores;
- Images: paintings, drawings, prints, photographs, pictures of museum objects, maps, graphic designs, plans and musical notation;

---

[13] Europeana Factsheet: <http://ec.europa.eu/information_society/doc/factsheets/071-europeana-en.pdf>

[14] <http://version1.europeana.eu/web/europeana-foundation/introduction>

[15] <http://mek.oszk.hu/00400/00485/00485.doc>

- Videos: films, news broadcasts and television programmes;
- Sound: music and spoken word from cylinders, tapes, discs and radio broadcasts;

These rich, but varied resources are managed by a series of organisational systems that are built into the architecture, such as vocabularies, thesauri, taxonomies, or other classification schemes. Organising the content in this way allows for the wealth of millions of objects to take up their logical place the system and facilitates searching the content using the Who – Where – When and What? – paradigms. The background semantic layer is, in fact, the key to true interoperability and this is what makes Europeana's content accessible, useable and exploitable. In the case of Europeana, the platform uses the SKOS standard (Simple Knowledge Organisation System)[16] as a common data model that shares and links knowledge via the Semantic Web by capturing the internal rules, making them explicit and sharing them across the whole platform. Once discovered, users can log in to Europeana to save their selections in "My Europeana" where items, searches and tags are saved by the user for future reference.

In order to facilitate the orderly flow of information into Europeana from different kinds of institutions across Europe, the EDL Foundation has created series of networks catering to the different sectors of Europe's cultural heritage holdings.

- *APEnet* aggregates content from Europe's national archives;
- *ATHENA* aggregates museum content and promotes standards for museum digitisation and metadata;
- *BHL-Europe* brings biodiversity heritage into Europeana;
- *Europeana Connect* adds sound material to Europeana;
- *European Film Gateway (EFG)* aggregates cinema related material;
- *Europeana Local* brings content from regional and local content holders;
- *EUscreen* contributes television material to Europeana;
- *Europeana Travel* will bring material associated with travel, trade, tourism and migration into Europeana;
- *Judaica Europeana* looks at the Jewish contribution to Europe's cultural heritage;
- *MIMO* will create a single access point to digital content and information musical instruments in European museums.

Two more partners have taken on specific responsibilities in the Europeana matrix: *Europeana Connect* which delivers technologies and resources to improve Europeana services, and *PrestoPRIME* which tackles long-term preservation of digital audiovisual material.

---

[16] <http://www.w3.org/TR/2008/WD-skos-reference-20080125>

Of particular interest to the museum community is ATHENA (Access to cultural heritage networks across Europe)[17] an eContentPlus Best Practice Network targeting the museums' sector and aiming at establishing conditions for lowering the barrier for museums to make their digital content accessible via Europeana. Led by Italian Ministry of Cultural Heritage, ATHENA is the network that takes on the responsibility of harvesting Europe's museums holdings, and facilitates their integration into Europeana. ATHENA's responsibilities (in tandem with other Europeana networks) include first and foremost a complex mapping of distributed objects across Europe, as well as the development of technical solutions; such as the proprietary ingestion tools that facilitate the seamless integration of holdings into the European Digital Library. In addition, ATHENA has taken on the responsibility to develop the standards, agreed upon by the museum community across Europe, into a coherent system of schema and standards for museums across Europe.

Clearly the European museum landscape is rich in a great variety of standards, necessitating a coherent policy and interoperability of standards. A survey has been carried out by Working Group 3 of ATHENA and the results have already been released; a comprehensive publication that is one of the many of the project's milestone deliverables. The publication describes the analysis and comparison of existing dictionaries, terminologies, thesauri, classifications, taxonomies etc. used by museums in a cross-domain perspective, which will be consequently compared with those adopted by the other sectors of cultural heritage, in order to facilitate the synchronization and integration of cultural holdings across the different sectors as they are ingested into Europeana. The standards currently under discussion are:

- CDWA lite-xsd-public-v1-1.xsd[18]
- museumdat-v1.0.xsd[19]
- spectrum-3.1.xsd[20]
- LIDO (Lightweight information describing objects – currently v0.7) to be launched in the spring of 2010.[21]

---

[17] See the article of Rossella Caffo in this publication.

[18] CDWA Lite is an XML schema to describe core records for works of art and material culture based on the *Categories for the Description of Works of Art* (CDWA) and *Cataloging Cultural Objects: A Guide to Describing Cultural Works and Their Images* (CCO) <http://www.getty.edu/research/conducting_research/standards/cdwa/cdwalite.html>

[19] *museumdat* is a harvesting format, optimised for retrieval and publication and meant to deliver automatically core data to museum portals. It builds largely upon the data format CDWA Lite developed in the US by the Getty, the Visual Resources Association and others, with a specific focus on arts. *museumdat* now applies for all kinds of object classes, e.g. cultural, technology or natural history, and is compatible with the reference model of the international documentation committee CIDOC-CRM (ISO 21127). *museumdat* is an outcome of the work of Fachgruppe Dokumentation des Deutschen Museumsbundes (DMB). <http://www.museumdat.org>

[20] SPECTRUM: <http://www.collectionstrust.org.uk/spectrum>

Reaching across Europe's museum community and defining it as a truly Pan-European project is dependent on the leadership from all of the nation states. ATHENA has therefore created a series of National Contact Points, each taking on a leadership role in their own country and currently include most of the European member states: Belgium, Bulgaria, Cyprus, Czech Republic, Estonia, Finland, France, Germany, Greece, Hungary, Italy, Latvia, Luxembourg, Malta, the Netherlands, Poland, Romania, Slovak Republic, Slovenia, Sweden, and the United Kingdom. In addition Azerbaijan, Israel, and Russia, as associate members are also harvesting their collections into Europeana via ATHENA. The call is still open and museums interested in joining the ATHENA Network are invited to contact their National Contact Point.[22] ATHENA builds on and continues the work previously realised by the MINERVA network,[23] a similar pan-European network that succeeded over recent years to increase awareness about best practices in digitisation, and acted to stimulate access to digital content among European cultural heritage professionals.

While, at the time of writing, Europeana is still in its early stage of development, and while it is in fact currently facing significant technical and usability challenges, it does promise to be an extremely ambitious digital library and one that is well poised to deliver quality cultural content from Europe's memory institutions. Even at this early stage Europeana has already won the *Erasmus EuroMedia Award* for Networking Europe.
Quoting the Erasmus announcement:

> "The website Europeana.eu is a surprising innovative interactive educational virtual exhibition in the field of the European cultural inheritance in the broadest sense of this container term."[24]

With this kind of recognition, Europeana has clearly a head start in digitising Europe's cultural heritage and with all the teams behind the scenes, each making their contribution, Europeana also seems to have a very promising future.

THE WORLD DIGITAL LIBRARY, UNESCO

In contrast to the ambitious quantity of content proposed for Europeana, UNESCO's World Digital Library (WDL)[25] represents a shift (in their words)

---

[21] LIDO, Lightweight Information Describing Objects: <http://museums.wikia.com/wiki/Berliner_Herbsttreffen_zur_Museumsdokumentation_2009>

[22] National Contact Points, <http://www.athenaeurope.org/index.php?en/132/national-contact-points>

[23] The MINERVA Europe Network: < www.minervaeurope.org>

[24] Erasmus EuroMedia Award for Networking Europe: <http://www.univie.ac.at/esec/php/wordpress/?page_id=5>

[25] The World Digital Library: < http://www.wdl.org/en>. See also the article of John Van Oudenaeren in this publication.

in digital library projects from a focus on quantity – for its own sake – to quality. Working with IFLA, UNESCO describes the objectives of the World Digital Library as promoting international and inter-cultural understanding and awareness, as well as a provision of resources to educators and scholarly research. In their additional goal to expand non-English and non-Western content on the Internet, the WDL has developed its approach to multilingualism by publishing the library in Arabic, Chinese, English, French, Portuguese, Russian, and Spanish. According to the WDL website[26] the governing board of the WDL noted that there was little cultural content being digitised in many countries and that developing countries in particular lacked the capacity to digitise and display their cultural treasures. They argued that existing websites often had poorly developed search and display functions, and that multilingual access was not well developed. In order to remedy these perceived inadequacies, the WDL, developed by a team at the Library of Congress, with technical assistance provided by the Bibliotheca Alexandrina of Alexandria in Egypt, was designed to identify, retrieve and present quality cultural content from all over the world.

The WDL has already made an example collection of high quality, primary materials, available from cultures around the world. The collection includes: manuscripts, maps, rare books, musical scores, recordings, films, prints, photographs, architectural drawings, and other significant cultural materials. Unlike Europeana that points to external content providers to display the collections, the WDL draws the high resolution objects directly into its architecture, taking over responsibility for consistent metadata, and promising persistent identifiers embedded within the system.

In addition to a free text search, users can browse the WDL by place, time, topic, type of item and institution. Each search offers a distinct pathway across the data, resulting in a display that is at the same time intuitive, effective and strikingly beautiful and promises a highly satisfying result on every kind of search.

THE WORLD DIGITAL LIBRARY

While the WDL is searchable in seven languages, it includes content in more than 40 languages from over 20 countries: Brazil, Egypt, China, France, Iraq, Israel, Japan, Mali, Mexico, Morocco, the Netherlands, Qatar, the Russian Federation, Saudi Arabia, Serbia, Slovakia, South Africa, Sweden, Uganda, the U.K., and the U.S.

---

[26] Background: <http://www.wdl.org/en/about/background.html>

The WDL has evolved from UNESCO's *Memory of the World* register[27] that lists documentary heritage, recommended by the International Advisory Committee, and endorsed by the Director-General of UNESCO, as corresponding to the selection criteria regarding world significance, and outstanding universal value. The programme was launched in 1992. Amongst the stated goals of the programme was to safeguard, protect and facilitate access to and the use of documentary heritage, especially heritage that is rare and endangered, and to guard them against collective amnesia.[28] Bringing these significant cultural holdings together in this way, and making them accessible to all, has already made a considerable contribution towards revealing some of the world's hidden treasures. As the WDL develops in depth and breath, more and more of the world's wonders will be thrust into the spotlight. And the library will continue to grow from strength to strength. In this way the WDL will evolve into an impressive centralised resource that greatly contributes rich cultural content to educators, and its wealth of high quality primary resources to scholarly research.

THE INTERNET ARCHIVE

So many new pages arrive online every day, and so much content is appearing on these pages, that it would take a mammoth library to contain all this content, and to maintain some sort of footprint to be preserved for the future. In a new evocation of a library – the digital library – *the Internet Archive (IA)* has been conceived, and developed for this specific goal. With a mandate to take a snapshot of all web pages on every website since 1996, this is truly a rethink of the term "library", but one that makes sense for the 21st Century! The IA is a non-profit organisation, dedicated to building and maintaining an archive of the Web that is free and openly accessible as an online digital library. The archive includes "snapshots of the World Wide Web" (archived copies of pages, taken at various points in time), to include: software, movies, books, and audio recordings. As a fully functioning library, the IA is a member of the American Library Association, and is officially recognized by the State of California as a library; making its collections permanently available at no cost to researchers, historians, scholars, and the general public.

The "Wayback Machine" is a digital time capsule created by the IA, that allows users to discover archived versions of web pages across time – what the Archive calls a "three dimensional index". In 2009 the *Wayback Machine* contained about 3 petabytes of data and was growing at a rate of 100 terabytes per

---

[27] <http://portal.unesco.org/ci/en/ev.php-URL_ID=17534&URL_DO=DO_TOPIC&URL_SECTION=201.html>

[28] Memory of the World Committee for Asia/Pacific: <http://www.unesco.mowcap.org>

month. This in fact reflects a growth rate that eclipses the amount of text contained in the world's largest libraries, including the Library of Congress – a truly remarkable achievement! There are currently over 10 billion web pages from over 16 million different sites stored on Petabox rack systems, manufactured by Capricorn Technologies.[29]

The *Internet Archive Project* was founded by Brewster Kahle as a "501(c)(3) non-profit" in 1996, in collaboration with large institutions such as the Library of Congress and the Smithsonian. Together they are working to preserve a record for generations to come, in order to prevent the Internet, and other "born digital" materials from disappearing into the past.[30] To ensure the stability and endurance of the *IA*, its collection is mirrored at the Bibliotheca Alexandrina in Egypt, an ancient center of learning that was said to contain a copy of every book in the world, but that was evidently burned to the ground.[31] For those of us with a short memory, we can now easily pop back to the past to retrieve websites and content that has long ago slipped out of Google's reach, as pages upon precious pages have long over-written their predecessors. Luckily for us, websites now can never really be lost, and content that was once interesting but perhaps has since lost its luster, or has simple been replaced by a fresher, sparklingly-newer version can now be retrieved with ease, saved locally, or re-uploaded online for others to share.

GOOGLE BOOKS

No search for the ultimate digital library would be possible without the inclusion of *Google Books*, the brand-name library, where readers can browse, search and read the full text of books – at least those books which are out of copyright, or those on which the publisher (Google has currently partnered with over 20,000 publishers and authors)[32] has given *Google Books* permission to upload it into their online collection.

Readers will then be able to see a preview of the book and in some cases the entire text (as long as it is in the public domain). Once copyright restrictions have been removed, you are free to download the book as a PDF copy.

The sense of free access is usually misleading, as in fact, what you can do when you locate your favourite author online is to discover that you can "learn about your book" is generally a euphemism for where you can borrow it from a library or, in most cases to find out where you can buy it online (one

---

[29] Capricorn Technologies: <http://www.capricorn-tech.com/casestudy_internetarchive.php>
[30] About the Internet Archive: <http://www.archive.org/about/about.php>
[31] The International School of Information Science (ISIS) research institute was founded in order to maximize creativity and foster innovations within the Bibliotheca Alexandrina (BA): <http://archive.bibalex.org>
[32] Google Books Settlement Agreement:<http://books.google.com/googlebooks/agreement>

click away). This is disappointing for the reader who gets to read only snippets of the full text – just as an appetizer – but it can be reassuring for the author who is concerned about losing the royalties from sales of the book!

These kind of copyright discussions have been raging for years since Google was sued in 2005 by the Authors Guild and the Association of American Publishers, who had claimed that Google Books violated copyright law. More recently, the company was taken to court in France over accusations that it was illegally reproducing and distributing copyrighted material as part of its project. On 19 November 2009 the Court granted preliminary approval of the Amended Settlement based and of the "13th November Agreement" that clarified the non-English books question, when the agreement specified that only published works from the US, UK, Australia and Canada will be included in Google's digital book search project.

The European Commission has joined in the ongoing discussion, and continues to support the digitisation and online accessibility of Europe's cultural heritage through Europeana, despite the technical and usability challenges the platform currently faces. The discussions rage on; with the ownership and management of cultural heritage at the heart of the arguments.

Even though people are often wary how ubiquitous Google has become, and how much it is already influencing and even directing our lives, the Mountain View company is continuing to develop platform upon platform to make our life just that more "Googlish". Adding just one more app to your mobile phone – as long as you are running an Android 1.6 that is – allows you to take a photo of any book you might notice on a friends coffee table or office desk, scan the image or text on the fly, and, with one click be taken to the online point of sale – providing it is either Google Books or another Google point of sale, such as their evolving print-on-demand service.

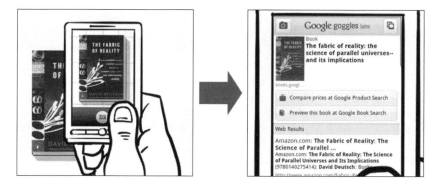

Graphic 2: <http://www.google.com/intl/it_ALL/mobile/google-mobile-app/>

It seems that there is a lot at stake when we unpack what is happening to various digital libraries that are currently under construction. It appears that they are provoking more than simple accessibility issues and are in fact cutting to the very core of who is responsible for managing the primary resources of our cultural selves – the books, works of art, music and films – that makes us who we are. Questions about who directs the cultural industries: the government or the private industry, become critical to what becomes available and accessible, and copyright issues in fact arise, that are not simply about micro-arguments between author and publisher, but have a far more global reach.

GOVERNMENT, INDUSTRY OR THE FOLK?

In addition to the two major players on the global platform, the top down governmental or private industry management of digital cultural heritage, the Web 2.0 platforms, now have to configure into a third actor: the folk – that is: you and me! With the power of the prosumer at our fingertips, we are now able to publish our own books, upload our favourite images, share our preferred music and video collections – even open up our online diaries – allowing others to sift, search and access our micro-content, while, at the same time we may access theirs. Web 2.0 now offers many different kinds of opportunities for the *folk* (you and me) to forge new horizontal connections with like-minded colleagues, friends, fans and business partners. Once connected, we can make our voice heard in new, creative ways. Through innovative collaborations we are able to become involved in new kinds of activities that are opening up for the cultural institutions and their public. Against this backdrop libraries are beginning to stake their claim, not only on their institutional website, and are also reinventing themselves across social networks, and, in doing so, are reaching out the public who expect to take on an active role in all that is happening.

This next section, rather than offering an exhaustive report on the technological solutions of Web 2.0 platforms, discusses the perspective of the user, and describes a series of case studies, particularly by the Nebraska State Library and the ecologies of Web 2.0 participation. It explores what it means to be an active participant in the authoring and disseminating personalised micro-content in a relationship with a cultural institution, an institution that has mostly acted – until recently – from within the traditional broadcast model approach.

BLOGS

The best known of the Web 2.0 platforms is the blog, a hybrid between a diary and an on-line journal, characterised by chronological ordering of information. The horizontal network of blogs that are interconnected through the embedded interface is known as "blogosphere" and with the blog platform being so simple to build and use, many institutions take up blogging as a way to present themselves online, rather than the more sophisticated building and development of a formal website. The added benefit here, of course, is the ability to be able to receive responses from the public, and in this way to be able to hold "conversations" with their public. The Nebraska Library Commission has an impressive series of such Web 2.0 conversations with their public over blogs, wikis and Twitter. [33]In each case the conversation takes on a specific rhythm, but in contrast to the traditional one way dissemination of information in traditional Web 1.0 services, these new conversations change the dynamic of the relationship between the library and the public. People soon learn to take on a more active role; such as taking part in Webinars, or learning to set up and run their own virtual meetings.

These kinds of discussions may be on the future of the printed book, or on how to find and use online state services for educational or medical needs. According to the Nebraska State Library website

"Nebraska Learns 2.0 is an ongoing self-discovery program which encourages participants to take control of their own learning and to utilize their lifelong learning skills through exploration and PLAY. The goal of the program is to encourage participants to experiment with and learn about the new and emerging technologies that are reshaping the way people, society and libraries access information and communicate with each other."

WIKIS

Taking this approach a stage forward – the Nebraska State Library is also using wikis to extend this conversation. A wiki (from a term in the Hawaiian language that means "very fast"), is a website (or a collection of hypertext documents) that can be both read as modified by its readers. The content of a wiki is developed in cooperation with all those who have access to it. The modification of the content is open and free, but it is organised chronologically and new content is added at the top. The aim of a wiki is the sharing, exchanging, storing and optimizing of knowledge in an atmosphere of cooperation. The Nebraska Overdrive Libraries has built a wiki in order to share their growing collection of digital audio books through Digital Library Reserve. The service is available to patrons of participating libraries through the Overdrive/DLR system and is designed for remote use by library patrons where they can access the digital materials via the web, or by download to Overdrive Download Stations in the physical library.

---

[33] Nebraska libraries: <http://www.librarysites.info/states/ne.htm>

FLICKR

The popular photo-sharing platform Flickr has become "the place" for professionals and amateurs alike, to post and share their photographic favourites. Moving into this highly social network, the Library of Congress has created their own space and has uploaded some 4,880 of its 14 million pictures to Flickr; in addition to their institutional website. Calling to the public to help them in identifying the images when their own information is limited, the Library of Congress welcomes the public's contribution of names, descriptions, locations, tags, and also their general reactions.[34]

The Library of Congress currently has two collections located on Flickr: *Historic Photos: 1930s-40s in colour* and Historic Newspapers; *News in the 1910s.*

According to Flickr:

"These beautiful, historic pictures from the Library represent materials for which the Library is not the intellectual property owner. *Flickr* is working with the Library of Congress to provide an appropriate statement for these materials. It's called '*no known copyright restrictions*'. Hopefully, this pilot can be used as a model that other cultural institutions would pick up, to share and redistribute the myriad collections held by cultural heritage institutions all over the world".

FACEBOOK

One of the more popular social networking sites is Facebook, and as well as the millions of individuals already active with their own Facebook page, we also can discover hundreds of thousands of memory institutions signing up to their own Facebook Page or Fan Group. There must be hundreds of libraries on Facebook, including many public and national libraries. Facebook was first conceived as social networking directory for Harvard students. As social connections naturally extended beyond the Harvard campus, so their online network quickly grew. The idea behind the network was taken from the printed book of faces that is distributed across campuses. These in-campus publications were designed so that students could get to know one another by reading about one another and to be able to recognise fellow students from their photos. Today, even those without the previously indispensable .edu or .ac email account can sign up and maintain daily or even hourly contact with their own personal network. There are hundreds of mini applications available to embed into the in-

---

[34] Screenshot of the Library of Congress Flickr Page: <www.flickr.com/photos/library_of_congress/collections>

terface. With a simple click you can add hundreds of different "gizmos" to your own home page, and some 140 museums on Facebook. Libraries have taken to Facebook as a means to reach their audiences and an additional space for conversations with the public.

TWITTER

Twitter is a micro-blogging interface that allows you to send "tweets"; text-based posts, up to 140 characters in length. These kinds of sites aim to keep you in touch with your own network; and if your network extends to your local library, you may wish to sign up and list to the tweets that fly back and forth between the library and the public. Here again, the Nebraska State Library has set up yet another opportunity to reach its public; a Twitter feed with some 400 people following the libraries' activities on a daily, if not hourly bases. At the same time the Commission is listening in to some 97 Tweet feeds, to keep up with the conversation that is going on in the field.[35]

CONCLUSIONS

Web 1.0 laid the rich foundation for libraries to move into Web 2.0 platforms where they discovered that their services could become far more user inclusive and far more responsive and interactive. They have not only opened up the authoring of content from meta to micro-content, they also have shifted the sites of knowledge authorship; and, in doing so, have caused tectonic shifts in the balance of power, associated with knowledge management. As the traditional wardens of not only the physical collections, but also the knowledge articulated by the collections, cultural institutions now have to pause to consider, both how to navigate web 2.0, as well as how to join in the synergy of social networking. These spaces cannot simply be ignored by cultural institutions; they are already taking up vast tracts of the World Wide Web. According to *Technorati*[36] at the beginning of 2008 they were tracking some 112.8 million blogs, and monitoring over 250 million pieces of tagged social media. This represents millions of conversations that are taking place outside of traditional web spaces. As a paradigm shift in the way we think about the World Wide Web, there is no going back. On March 15, 2007, wiki entered the Oxford English Dictionary Online,[37] and as knowledge resources are articulated by wiki environments, we too are becoming accustomed to the fact that it is not always the traditional institution that is a steward for the conversations.

---

[35] Screenhot: Nebraska Library Commission on Twitter <http://twitter.com/NLC_Reference>

[36] <http://technorati.com/>

[37] <http://www.oed.com/>

In this kind of environment people are searching for books and with the various electronic readers now available, once they are wifi enabled, you can download any book, anytime, anywhere. If you are reading your favourite book on your mobile reader, why would you even need a library in the first place? According to the Gutenberg Project website there are already 2,320,000 eBooks online.

1,550,000 Internet Archive
500,000 World Public Library[38]
113,000 Project Gutenberg
130,000 ebooksabouteverything.com[39]
37,000 Other eBook Sites

2,320,000 Grand Total [Estimate][40]

This kind of online access is clearly bypassing traditional libraries and taking into consideration the time people spend in conversation with each other online, if the library does not make this leap of faith into the digital realm – and especially the Web 2.0 arena – they will surely be left out of the race.

Even discussions on library collections are taking place online. With some 900,000 member, Library Thing,[41] the social network space which intrinsically acts as the world's largest book club, you can catalogue your books and share your collections and tastes in literature with others; in fact, Library Thing acts as a resource for librarians as well as for book lovers.

The move to the digital library is not only affecting the library profession; all of the cultural industries are experiencing similar paradigm shifts, as are the professions of journalism, museums, and traditional broadcast media. This is truly an interesting time, and tracking what is happening to the library professional is still very much an open book.

---

[38] <http://worldlibrary.net/>
[39] <http://www.diesel-ebooks.com/>
[40] Gutenberg Project News: <http://www.gutenbergnews.org/>
[41] Library Thing: http://www.librarything.com/>

SESSION 3

STRATEGIES FOR INSTITUTIONS: RESPONDING TO THE DIGITAL CHALLENGE

TO MAKE A BETTER DIGITAL LIBRARY – SOME COLLABORATIVE EFFORTS IN CHINA

Zhu Qiang

ABSTRACT

The digital library is facing some bottleneck issues in China, such as duplication of digitisation, standardisation, intellectual property protection, digital preservation, etc. Two kinds of mechanism have been set up to do some coordination and exploration to solve these issues. So far they've played some good roles in digital library construction and service.

DIGITAL LIBRARY ACHIEVEMENTS IN CHINA

In China we make a distinction between two kinds of digital library initiatives: on the one hand the for-profit initiatives, resulting in digital libraries that are made by digital content and service providers, publishers etc., and on the other hand the non-for-profit initiatives, resulting in libraries made by libraries or governmental and public sectors. At the same time we distinguish a few levels on which digital libraries are created: a national level, a provincial/regional level and a single library/multi-libraries level.

There are several national-level digital library projects I would like to mention here as an example:

- 1997, China Pilot Digital Library Project;
- 1998, CALIS (China Academic Library & Information System);
- 1999, NSDL (National Science Digital Library);
- 2000, NSTL (National Science and Technology Library);
- 2001, National Digital Library of China

Throughout the preparation and the building phases, various activities have been undertaken in cooperation. Cooperation took place in the form of large-scale cooperative purchasing, for instance for CALIS, CAS (Chinese Academy of Science) and for various digital libraries of local universities/colleges; in large scale digitisation, for instance in the case of the NDL (National Digital Library) and CADAL (China-US Million Book Digital Library Project) and in large-scale database development, for instance in the case of CALIS and NSTL.

Over all, one could say that the building of digital libraries is no longer a trend in China. It is a growing reality around us, and we experience that to a growing extend, the digital libraries play a positive role in people's daily work, study and life.

CHALLENGES OF FURTHER DEVELOPMENTS

In further developing digital library initiatives, we are facing several bottle-necks: we meet the risk of duplicating development issues in the area of digiti-sation and database building; we have to deal with the digital copyright issue; with formulating standards and criteria and we have to take care of long-term preservation of the digitised material that is available through our digital libraries.

Qihao Miao, the vice-director of the Shanghai Library, summarized the challenges we stand for in the following way:

"At the first beginning, the digital library in China was established from the technology point of view. However, the problems now mainly con-centrate at the management level. Objectively speaking, today's problems just reflect our progress."

STRENGTHENING MACRO CONTROL

To provide for a mechanism and measures to strengthen the macro control of digital libraries in China, the initiative was taken to found the *Joint Meeting on Digital Library Development and Services in China*.[1] This meeting aims to strengthen the cooperation and sharing of digital libraries. The following libraries and institutions are members of the Joint Meeting:

- NLC (National Library of China);
- NCIRSP (National Cultural Information Resources Sharing Project);
- CALIS (China Academic Library & Information System);
- Shanghai Library;
- NSL (National Science Library, CAS);
- Library of Party School of the Central Committee of C.P.C;
- Library of National Defense University;
- Zhejiang University Library.

---

[1] <http://jcdl.org/>

JOINT MEETING ON DIGITIAL LIBRARY DEVELOPMENT AND SERVICES IN CHINA

How does the Joint Meeting operates? Both the Department of Community Culture of the Ministry of Culture and the Secretariat of the Library Society of China play an organising role in the Joint Meeting. The Meeting is generally held quarterly, but it can also be convened according to the needs of members and by common agreement of the members. Each meeting is funded and operated by another member. The first round of meetings was planned as follows:

- First meeting: NLC, July 2007, Beijing;
- Second meeting: CALIS & CADAL, October 2007, Fenghua;
- Third meeting: Shanghai Library, January 2008, Shanghai;
- Fourth meeting: Library of Party School of the Central Committee of C.P.C, April 2008;
- Fifth meeting: NSL.CAS, July 2008;
- Sixth meeting: National Cultural Information Resources; Administrative Center, October 2008, Beijing;
- Seventh meeting: Library of National Defense University, January 2009, Beijing.

Each Joint Meeting is centralized around one main theme. The First meeting focused on the current status of communication; discussed questions on release and discussed the Joint Meeting mechanism establishment.

The Second meeting covered the definition of functions and the settlement of problems. At the Third meeting the topics were: publicity and promotion; discussion on ongoing projects (recommended standards and criteria). During the Third Meeting a cooperative agreement was signed by the NLC and the Shanghai Library. At the Fourth meeting, the central focal point was the investigation of and discussion on resources and documents discussion and at this occasion a second cooperative agreement was signed by NCIRSP and Library of Party School of the C.C.C.P.C. At the Fifth meeting we reviewed the achievements of activities in 2007 and 2008. A third agreement was signed by the NLC and CADAL. At the Sixth meeting we were able to release the application system, to settle the communication around service policies and we finally were able to display the Digital Library achievements.

At the Seventh meeting we continued the discussion on service policies; brochures were compiled and a fourth agreement was signed, now by NCIRSP, NSL and CADAL. At the Eighth meeting of the Joint Meeting we plan to release the draft of the Service Policy Guidelines release and we hope to continue the discussion on resource processing.[2]

---

[2]   Website <http://www.lsc.org.cn/CN/stlxhy.html> (Chinese)

I would like to end this introduction of the Joint Meeting by summarizing the main achievements of this initiative up till now. We have produced three major documents: a draft on Recommended Standards and Criteria of Chinese Digital Library; a draft version of the Service Policy Guidelines and a general brochure on the achievements of Digital Library development. We also have delivered two application systems: a Registration & Navigation System of Digital Library Resources and a Recommended System of Chinese Digital Library Standards and Criteria.

THE HIGH-LEVEL FORUM ON DIGITAL LIBRARIES

A second initiative to provide for a mechanism and measures to strengthen the macro control of digital libraries was the founding of the High-Level Forum on Digital Libraries in China in 2008. This Forum was initiated by NSTL and included the experts from professional libraries, academic libraries, public libraries and the institutions of relevant fields (information service and technology, laws, etc.).

The High-Level Forum aims to promote the communication among the institutions about their strategic study and planning on digital libraries. It focuses on important development trends of the network information environment and on information services; on models of modern information development and literature services and on the development of strategies of library and information service.

This is how the High-Forum mechanism works. It is operated by the Organizing Committee (that is appointed every four years) and the secretariat. The Forum is held annually or twice a year and again, each Forum has a specific theme. For every Forum 1-3 Chairmen are selected. The chairmen are responsible for the organisation of the meeting and for choosing of the topic.
Detailed content on the High-Level Forum on Digital Libraries in China can be found on the website.[3]

The First Annual Meeting of the High Forum took place in Beijing in 2008. The central theme was: "The service system development of long-term preservation of digital resources in China". After the keynote report by Qiheng Hu and further relevant reports by selected delegates, a discussion followed on the central theme.

The First Annual Meeting resulted in a Declaration of Action on Long-term Preservation of Digital Resources including the following calls:

– Call on the initiation of action on long-term preservation of digital resources by Chinese government;

---

[3]   Website <http://dlforum.org.cn/index.jsp> (Chinese)

- Call on the development of storage system on long-term preservation of digital resources under government support;
- Call on the promotion of laws, policies and mechanism on long-term preservation of digital resources by relevant experts.

The Declaration was signed by all participants in person.

The Second Annual Meeting will be held in 2009 in Shanghai on the theme: "Digital Library coordinated service mechanism and its implementation strategy". For the programme we have planned a Keynote report by Xiaolin Zhang and relevant reports by six or seven selected speakers, followed by a discussion.

CONCLUSIONS

Overseeing the recent developments on digital libraries in China in the recent years, a set of preferred conditions for a Digital Library can be formulated:

- The development of a Digital Library ideally should start from reality;
- The development of a Digital Library should strengthen the top-level design;
- Any Digital Library project should focus on resource sharing and cooperation;
- A Digital Library should be widely open: not only built with an open source code and built with open applications, but also in providing open access to literature resources;
- A Digital Library stimulates cooperation with the computer community, the publishing field and the users.

STRATEGIES FOR INSTITUTIONS:
RESPONDING TO THE DIGITAL CHALLENGE

Rossella Caffo

ABSTRACT

For many years the Central Institute for the Union Catalogue of the Italian Libraries (ICCU) has been involved in the coordination of European and national projects that promote the digitisation and online accessibility of cultural heritage. The main national initiatives are: the National Library Service SBN; Internet Culturale; CulturaItalia. Among the European projects it is worth mentioning: MINERVA; MICHAEL; ATHENA. All these initiatives share a distributed approach, coordination structures at local, regional, and national level, tight liaisons with national digitisation strategies, the active participation of thousands of cultural institutions at every level and sector, and, last but not least, a cross domain approach. Together they foster at the national and European level a positive attitude among archives, libraries, museums. All these efforts have produced a wide range of benefits for stakeholders, including administrations, institutions, users. Collectively, these initiatives have multiplied the methods of access, fostered interoperability of systems, and promoted local initiatives.

In 2008, the Italian Ministry of Cultural Heritage and Activities, Istituto Centrale per il Catalogo Unico delle Biblioteche Italiane encouraged IFLA to organise a conference focusing on digital library users. The proposal was made while considering the valuable experience gained while coordinating important European projects such as MINERVA and MICHAEL in the framework of digital cultural heritage.

This contribution intents to explain digital library strategies at the national and European level that were adopted by the Italian Ministry of Cultural Heritage and Activities in order to coordinate digitisation initiatives and to promote access to cultural information.

The Italian Ministry's strategy is focusing on the integration of existing information systems, on the recovery of databases not in line with current international standards, the creation of web sites and cultural portals.

ICCU

The Central Institute for the Union Catalogue of Italian Libraries and for Bibliographic Information (ICCU) is the institute coordinating all cataloguing and documentation activities carried out by Italian libraries. ICCU promotes and develops programmes, studies and scientific initiatives concerning cataloguing, inventories and digitisation of the bibliographic and documentary heritage preserved in state libraries and other Italian public and private institutions. ICCU coordinates the development and dissemination of the librarian's cultural heritage in order to define a national system of services.

Through the Technologic Observatory of Cultural Assets and Activities (OTEBAC) ICCU also promotes the harmonisation of digitisation standards and the management of digital resources across all sectors of cultural heritage.

In addition ICCU:

- coordinates, promotes and manages the catalogue, the network of the National Library Service (SBN), Interlibrary loan and documents delivery;
- coordinates, promote sand manages the national databases concerning the census, manuscripts, antique books and the Italian library database;
- promotes and coordinates the production of national regulations and the dissemination of international standards and cataloguing rules, assuring the uniformity of the catalogue and the production of bibliographic control;
- participates at international level in the production of bibliographic standards;
- promotes and coordinates standards for digitisation of bibliographic and documentary heritage, related to archiving, conservation and access resources;
- coordinates the monitoring of digitisation projects and oversees the publication and dissemination of digital resources, integrating them with SBN;
- manages education and training activities, offering traditional and online courses:
- takes part in international projects concerning the dissemination of information and digitisation of cultural and scientific heritage, such as ATHENA, CERL, DC-Net, DPE, MICHAEL, TEL, Europeana;
- Carries out editorial activities.

The activities, researches and technical actions are promoted by ICCU in accordance with the general directives of the Ministry of Cultural Heritage and Activities and of the General Directorate for Library Heritage, Cultural Institutes and Copyright.

What follows is a summary presentation of the most important projects monitored by ICCU.

SBN

SBN (Servizio bibliotecario nazionale, i.e. the Italian library network),[1] is an infrastructure of national services for users, promoted by the Ministry of Cul-

---

[1] <http://www.sbn.it>

tural Heritage and Activities and coordinated by ICCU in cooperation with Regions and Universities. State libraries as well as local, university and private libraries operating in different sectors are linked to the SBN.

The libraries participating in SBN (approximately 4.000) are organised in 65 nodes distributed across Italy and connected to a central system (the Index), which sets up the general catalogue of libraries belonging to the network.
In 2002, with the launching of the Index evolution project, the rationalisation, integration and renovation of the Index central database was developed and the opening to other systems and management of different levels of cooperation was also envisaged.

The main aims of the project were: the technological renewal of hardware and software; the opening of the SBN Index to management systems of a non-SBN library using the most widespread bibliographic formats (UNIMARC, MARC21); the management of diversified levels of cooperation; the development of new activities such as cataloguing of special materials; developing governance and monitoring functions, and increasing the number of databases.

Since 1997 the Index has been available to users through the OPAC (Online Public Access Catalogue) system that allows access to the content of the catalogue, with research methods that are user-friendly and articulated.

The OPAC database currently contains 10 million different pieces of information and 30 millions of holdings; it can be accessed using two portals[2] with approximately 20 million searches carried out annually.

Other important features of the OPAC SBN system across the Web are: the service of SBN ILL Interlibrary Loan; integration with the local OPACS; access to the cards of the identified libraries; presentation of search results in various formats among which UNIMARC and USMARC formats; UNIMARC export of individual bibliographic items; possibility of search and presentation for authority entries regarding authors included in the SBN Index (currently 36.000); the possibility to operate as a Z39.50 client and therefore to integrate other Z39.50 catalogues at a national and international level.

INTERNET CULTURALE

Internet Culturale is a multilingual portal (in Italian, English, French and Spanish) that allows users to access documents and digital resources of Italian libraries and to find information on their activities.

Through the portal, users can search within the national online loan service; visualize and download images of linked digital collections; access to the Inter Library Loan service; search in the digitised historical catalogues of Italian public institutions and search in the Italian libraries database.

---

[2]   <http://opac.sbn.it >or <http://www.internetculturale.it>

In the section devoted to special catalogues, users can find information on Italian editions of the 16th century (EDIT16); manuscripts in Latin owned by the libraries participating the Manus national census; the bibliography of manuscripts produced by the Institutions joining the BibMan project; the description and digital reproduction of Greek palimpsests.

Internet Culturale also allows browsing, with the help of three-dimensional technologies, of animations, hypertexts, through virtual exhibitions dedicated to famous characters (e.g. Svevo, Verdi, Totò) and tourist cultural itineraries or gourmet journeys.

Internet Culturale also devotes a large section to musical heritage, allowing the search by institutions, projects, collections, authors and by rare items such as autographs (there are for example 272 items on Donizzetti, 70 items on Puccini, 25 items on Bellini), by musical itineraries.

Contributions come from state libraries and monumental libraries, libraries of conservatories, museums, civic institutions, state archives, and important musical institutions.

The digital objects are almost all preserved in the ICCU repository with approximately one and a half million images, forming a rich online database.

The digitisation of the historical catalogues of libraries took place in the framework of the Italian Digital Library Project and includes the scanning, in image format, of over 200 Italian public library catalogues, making available about 7 millions images accessible through Internet Culturale.

This collection gathers digital reproductions of catalogues, in cards or in volumes, organised in different ways (alphabetic, topographic, systematic, and mixed) and related to various materials (printed editions, manuscripts, special materials). The headings were taken in the form in which they appear in the catalogue (without standardization) in order to respect the "historical authenticity" of the catalogues.

Information about libraries and about each digitised catalogue (history, organisation, special ways of searching) is also available.

Internet Culturale is integrated with CulturaItalia, the aggregator of content and access point to databases, websites and digital collections, involving all sectors of cultural heritage.

CULTURAITALIA

CulturaItalia[3] proposes guided access to the world of Italian culture. Thanks to innovative IT solutions, the portal gathers and organises millions of information-related elements on the resources that make up the country's vast cultural universe, and makes them available to all web users.

---

[3] <http://www.culturaitalia.it>

The data on cultural resources are not produced by the portal, but are provided directly by the entities that own and manage the resources. All the operators in the cultural sector – public administration and private companies – upload only the "metadata", that is, the descriptive information of the resources in their possession. CulturaItalia offers users the opportunity to consult and search information on Italian cultural resources within a single site.

The user, through the portal, accesses a database of "metadata" which gathers and organises the information arriving from all providers participating in CulturaItalia. Users can discover resources of all types which make up the country's extensive cultural heritage (museums, photographs, libraries, archives, galleries, exhibits, monuments, videos, discs, etc.), can carry out searches for scientific research or just out of simple curiosity. CulturaItalia is an "open" system that grows and develops in sync with the new information contained in the resources that enrich its database. The portal does not contain resources on Italian cultural heritage, but rather proposes itself as a starting point for a guided search towards other sites.

The portal offers a service to users, who will have at their disposal a single location from where to start their own search itineraries online, in terms of Italian culture, and the operators in the field, who can take advantage of a high-quality showcase to promote their own content. Once the resources of interest are located in CulturaItalia, the user can consult them directly at the data source, by heading to the provider's site or by contacting them via other channels, to complete the process of analysis and understanding.

The portal is an answer to the needs of an expert public as well as to the needs of the general public. CulturaItalia offers to specialised users, such as students, researchers, and those employed in the cultural sector, the opportunity to carry out targeted searches that correspond to very specific interests using very advanced software. For non-specialised users, such as citizens and tourists, the portal encourages curiosity and offers opportunities to discover or find out more about cultural resources available in the territory; this is possible because of its editorial content (thematic itineraries, articles, highlights, events, columns) published to spotlight the stores of "metadata" present in the website database.

The project is promoted and managed by the Ministry of Cultural Heritage and Activities (MiBAC) with the scientific consultation of the Scuola Normale Superiore of Pisa. CulturaItalia is supported by many organisations and institutions that belong to the world of Italian culture and provide the relevant information, that is to say: the real "primary resource" of the portal. Precisely because of its ability to integrate in one system the information-related elements of many different entities, CulturaItalia is a leading project in Europe and has been used as a reference for many other countries hoping to promote similar initiatives. CulturaItalia is the national aggregator which feeds Europeana, the European Digital Library. Recently CulturaItalia launched an online survey to measure users' satisfaction based on the Minerva *Handbook on cultural web user interaction (2008)*4.

When considering experiences at the European level, three projects come to mind and are worth mentioning: MINERVA, MICHAEL, and ATHENA. All three projects are coordinated by the Italian Ministry.

MINERVA

The MINERVA project[5], MInisterial NEtwoRk for Valorizing digitisation Activities was founded in 2002 in the framework of the IST Programme;[6] its goal was to create a network of European Ministries of Culture to discuss, correlate and harmonise the activities carried out in the field of digitisation of cultural content and to create a shared set of recommendations and guidelines on digitisation, metadata, interoperability and cultural websites. MINERVA operated from 2002 to 2008 through the coordination of national digitisation policies and programmes. It supported the National Representatives Group for digitisation (NRG)[7] in order to facilitate the creation of value added products and services shared at the European level, to improve the awareness of the existing state-of-the-art in the sector, to help overcome the fragmentation and duplication of digitisation activities of cultural and scientific content and to maximise cooperation among Member States. MINERVA was able to involve a growing number of countries – such as all the new Member States joining the European Union in 2004 through the project's extension MinervaPLUS – as well as many international organisations, associations, networks, national and international projects involved in this sector. Because of the high level of commitment assured by the involvement of governmental bodies, many national digitisation programmes were inspired to the MINERVA principles. In fact, MINERVA acted as a bridge between national initiatives and European policies.

Since October 2006, the MINERVA project was enlarged to MINERVAeC, MInisterial NEtwoRk for Valorising Activities in digitisation, eContentplus – supporting the European Digital Library. MINERVA eC was a thematic network in the area of cultural, scientific information and scholarly content. The consortium brought together stakeholders and experts from all over Europe, capitalising on the results achieved by the previous MINERVA projects, and supporting the European Commission initiative i2010 – Digital Libraries.

MINERVA worked in different fields: assessment and evaluation, awareness, dissemination and mobilisation of stakeholders, European cultural content inter-

---

[4]   MINERVA (2008), Handbook on cultural web user interaction <http://www.minervaeurope.org/publications/handbookwebusers.htm>

[5]   <http://www.minervaeurope.org>

[6]   <http://cordis.europa.eu/ist/>

[7]   <http://www.minervaeurope.org/structure/nrg.htm>

operability framework, quality, accessibility and usability, and best practices for content enrichment. MINERVA has produced several publications in order to disseminate the results of its working groups and NRG activities.[8]

Minerva contributed by stimulating decision makers and implementers to carrying out their initiatives of content enrichment, and to create the conditions needed to improve the quality of content and services as well as enhancing accessibility of digital content.

MICHAEL AND MICHAEL PLUS

The MICHAEL[9] and MICHAEL Plus projects were funded through the European Commission's e Ten programme,[10] to establish a new service for the European cultural heritage.

The MICHAEL project (Multilingual Inventory of Cultural Heritage in Europe) was a partnership between France, Italy and the UK, to deploy a cultural portal platform that was developed in France. MICHAEL Plus then extended the MICHAEL project to the Czech Republic, Finland, Germany, Greece, Hungary, Malta, the Netherlands, Poland, Portugal, Spain and Sweden. The two projects were closely aligned. The projects focused on the integration of national initiatives in digitisation of the cultural heritage and interoperability between national cultural portals, to promote access to digital content from museums, libraries and archives.

The projects have established this international online service, to allow users to search, browse and examine descriptions of resources held in institutions across Europe. We hope that the technical standards and sustainability model that we have established for the project will mean that more countries will provide their content to the portal in future times.

Through the multilingual MICHAEL service people are able to find and explore European digital cultural heritage materials by using the Internet. Michael's objectives were: a European cultural heritage inventory, available to all and providing access to cultural heritage resources; sustainable management for the project to continue; endorsement and implementation at a national gov-

---

[8] Progress reports of the National Representatives Group: coordination mechanisms for digitisation policies and programmes 2002, 2003, 2004, 2005, 2006, 2007; report on inventories and multilingualism issues: multilingualism and thesaurus; Guide to Intellectual Property Rights and Other Legal Issues; Handbook for quality in cultural websites: improving quality for citizens; Cultural Website Quality Principles and the relevant Handbook: Technical Guidelines for Digital Cultural Content Creation Programmes. At: <http://www.minervaeurope.org/ interoperability/technicalguidelines.htm>; *Handbook on cultural web user interaction; Cost reduction in digitisation.*

[9] <http://www.michael-culture.org>

[10] <http://ec.europa.eu/information_society/activities/eten/library/about/ leaflet/index_en.htm>

ernment level, in order to underpin further funding as required; a methodological and technical platform, which makes it easy to add new national instances of MICHAEL, thus improving the content and user bases.

The technical results of the MICHAEL project can be listed as follows: the MICHAEL data model for multilingual digital cultural heritage inventories; an open source technical platform for national instances built on Apache Tomcat, Cocoon, XtoGen, XML etc.; interoperability protocols for national instances to contribute data to the European service; European MICHAEL search portal; methodology and model which is easy to deploy in additional countries.

MICHAEL currently includes some 10.000 digital collections from 4.000 cultural institutions in Europe. The MICHAEL Consortium (19 states and 40 partners) has set up an international association known as MICHAEL-Culture AISBL, to grant sustainability and to allow for further service developments. MICHAEL-Culture is a member of the European Digital Library Foundation that manages and monitors the implementation of Europeana.

ATHENA

In November 2008, the "Network of Best Practice" was launched by the *eContentplus* programme.[11] This is a new project known as ATHENA (Access to Cultural Heritage Networks Across Europe)[12] developed by the MINERVA network. Its partners come from 20 EU Member States together with 3 non-European observers. 109 major museums and other cultural institutions are directly associated with the project, and 20 European languages are represented. It is coordinated by the Italian Ministry of Cultural Heritage.

ATHENA's objectives are to support and encourage the participation of museums and other institutions not yet fully involved in Europeana; and produce a set of scalable tools, recommendations and guidelines, focusing on multilingualism and semantics, metadata and thesauri, data structures and IPR issues. These will be used by museums to support internal digitization projects and to facilitate the integration of their digital content into Europeana; identify digital content that are present in European museums; contribute to the integration of the different sectors of cultural heritage with the overall objective to merge all these different contributions into Europeana. This will be carried out in cooperation with other projects more directly focused on libraries and archives; ATHENEA also develops a technical infrastructure that will enable semantic interoperability with Europeana.

ATHENA will bring together relevant stakeholders and content owners from all over Europe; evaluate and integrate standards and tools for facilitating the

---

[11] <http://ec.europa.eu/information_society/activities/econtentplus/index_en.htm>
[12] <http://www.athenaeurope.org>

inclusion of new digital content into Europeana; enable the user of Europeana to have a complete experience of European cultural heritage; work with existing projects (Europeana, and Michael are both present in ATHENA); and develop links and joint activities with other relevant projects in the Europeana "cluster" (for example EuropeanaLocal).[13]

CONCLUSIONS

All the noted initiatives have a common distributed approach, share coordination structures at local, regional and national level, have close links with national digitisation strategies, benefiting from the active participation of hundreds of cultural institutions (at all levels and in all sectors). Finally, they all have a cross-domain approach with museums, archives and libraries.

All these efforts have generated a number of benefits for all involved stakeholders: local administrations, institutions and end-users.
The modalities to access information have exponentially increased, interoperability is undergoing rapid changes, and local initiatives are enhanced thanks to new scenarios.

Furthermore, at Italian and European levels, many training courses focusing on all digitisation themes were organised at central level, but also in collaboration with local bodies and universities.

Let me conclude with the hope that there will soon be within IFLA a specific line of action devoted to digital libraries. The centuries old experience of libraries in organising the body of knowledge, existing in this sector, could be of great help for other institutions operating in the field of memory.

---

[13]   <http://www.europeanalocal.eu/>

STRATEGIES FOR INSTITUTIONS:
RESPONDING TO THE DIGITAL CHALLENGE:
THE WORLD DIGITAL LIBRARY PERSPECTIVE

John Van Oudenaeren

ABSTRACT

The digital information environment is characterized by factors that include: (1) increasing to near-total reliance of various user groups on electronic media for access to information, including cultural information; (2) growing impact of globalization and cross-national flows of information, combined with large and persisting disparities both within and between countries with regard to access to digital information and opportunities to create digital content; (3) proliferation and increasing diversity of devices on which digital content can be accessed; (4) growing importance of user participation in the creation and re-creation of digital content; (5) relative decline of the centrality of print and increased importance of audio and visual media; (6) key role of search engines and other mechanisms that provide fast access to vast amounts of information but that do so in ways that fragment and disaggregate information; (7) difficult economic circumstances and great uncertainty about the financial sustainability of both old and new media. The World Digital Library, a project launched by the Library of Congress in cooperation with UNESCO in 2005, has been planned and designed with many of these factors in mind. User feedback on the World Digital Library since its launch on 21 April 2009, validates many design and development decisions, as well as suggests areas for ongoing work.

To address the question of how libraries and other cultural institutions are responding or should respond to the digital challenge, this paper identifies seven general trends or sets of conditions that define the nature of this challenge. For each of these conditions, the paper identifies strategies that cultural institutions are taking to meet the digital challenge, focusing on those strategies that are most widely used and seem to offer the greatest promise of success. The paper concludes with a discussion of the World Digital Library <(www.wdl.org> as a particular response by the Library of Congress and its partner institutions to the digital challenge.

CURRENT CONDITIONS, STRATEGIC RESPONSES

The current digital environment is characterized by seven general trends or conditions:

- Increasing to near-total reliance of many users on electronic media for access to information;
- Problems of financial viability and sustainability in both old and new media;
- Globalization, but with persisting digital divides;
- Increasing diversity of ways to access digital content;
- A relative shift from text to audio and audio-visual media;
- The dominant role of search engines;
- Ever-rising user expectations.

ACCESS TO INFORMATION

It is often said that libraries in the digital age face the difficult task of having to operate in both the print and electronic worlds. This is indeed true, as vast numbers of paper books, newspapers, and other materials continue to be published and need to be acquired, catalogued, stored, and preserved, even as the universe of born digital or digitally-converted material continues to explode. The need to operate in both the paper and the digital world presents a major financial challenge for libraries, especially those charged with the care of large legacy collections.

The persistence of this duality should not obscure the fact, however, that for a growing number of people, especially the young people often characterized as "digital natives," no such duality exists. Information is accessed only in electronic form. If it cannot be accessed digitally, it does not exist for them.

A vast body of statistical and anecdotal evidence attests to this trend. Under the corporate motto of "organising the world's information", Google has set out to "digitize every book in the world" and is, by all accounts, making considerable progress toward achieving this objective. Not surprisingly, a growing number of readers have come to expect that it is only a matter of time before "everything is digitized."

Other indications of this trend include the ubiquitous problems in the old media (e.g., falling newspaper subscriptions), near-empty reading rooms in university and other libraries, and the rapid growth in the use of electronic book readers such as the Kindle. 2009 in fact may come to be seen as the "take off" year for these devices.

Libraries are responding to this aspect of the current environment in a variety of ways. First, and most fundamentally, they are going where the users are:

online. Libraries are attempting to digitise and place on the web more of their content, both books and special collections, as well as facilitate access to born digital materials that they control.

Paradoxically, efforts to digitise and place online additional content may be hampered somewhat by the very inexorability of the trends underway. Under the assumption that "everything is going to be online eventually anyway," foundations, government agencies, and corporations may be less interested in supporting digitisation efforts than they were, for example, in the 1990s, when digitisation was a newer and more glamorous technology.

Another strategic approach that libraries are taking is to deal with copyright and Intellectual Property issues in new ways. The development of the Creative Commons license[1] and new approaches to "best edition" (including requests for new or amended legislation in many countries to deal with electronic materials) are examples that come to mind.

A third strategy that libraries are adopting is to redefine their relationships with private industry. In the past, libraries purchased information from private companies (and non profit firms that functioned essentially as commercial companies, e.g., university presses) in the form of books, magazines, newspapers, and licensed databases, which they served to end users. They did not compete directly with these companies in presenting information to users. This is no longer the case, as advertising- and fee-based services by companies deal directly with readers and researchers. In this new environment, private companies are both partners (e.g., the libraries that work with Google in Google BookSearch) and competitors.

FINANCIAL VIABILITY AND SUSTAINABILITY

A second aspect of the current environment is the problem of financial viability and sustainability in both old and new media. Old media companies – book publishers, newspapers, music companies – are suffering, but many "new media" companies are having trouble as well. Talk of how to "monetize the Internet" is ubiquitous, with a large share of revenues and profits falling to a handful of companies with successful strategies (Google, Amazon, Apple). These financial challenges specific to the digital environment have arisen, moreover, against the backdrop of the difficult overall economic situation that has prevailed since 2008.

Financial challenges are affecting libraries in many ways. For many, it can mean fewer resources at a time of exploding work load. It also means a more difficult fundraising environment as foundations and other donors cut back giving or are compelled to devote resources to other pressing needs.

---

[1]   <http://creativecommons.org/>

Libraries are adopting a number of strategies to cope with financial and budgetary challenges. One is to cut back on legacy functions inherited from the pre-digital age, such as cataloguing, acquiring, and storing print materials and keeping open under-used reading rooms and information desks. Decisions to cut back in these areas are often made reluctantly and with a great deal of internal debate, but they nonetheless are being taken.

A second strategy is to redouble private fundraising efforts. A third is to develop partnerships with industry, the most notable of which are the library partnerships with Google for the mass digitisation of books. A fourth approach, one that cuts somewhat against the pursuit of private partnerships, is to assert the public good function of library involvement in digital activities (or, to put it differently, to emphasize the "public bad" of allowing private sector monopolization in this area) as a way of garnering increased support from governments and parliaments. This approach has been used with some success in Europe to generate national and EU-level support for projects aimed at countering the dominance of Google, but it could in principle be used elsewhere.

A final strategy, as yet largely unexplored but with great potential, is to tap into volunteer communities as a way of lowering costs and creating digital products that libraries otherwise could not afford to produce. This approach has been used to great effect by private companies (Flickr; YouTube) and could be tried more extensively in the non-profit cultural sector.

GLOBALISATION AND PERSISTING DIGITAL DIVIDES

A third general feature of the digital environment is globalization, which is occurring unevenly, with one result being the creation of persisting "digital divides." About 25 percent of the world's population has Internet access (for March 2009, an estimated 1.596 billion people out of a total world population of 6.710 billion), but penetration rates range from 74.4 percent in North America to 5.6 percent in Africa.[2] Disparities in access to broadband are even wider, and disparities with regard to content creation are wider still. English content is still dominant, but there is rapid growth in other languages, especially Chinese. Disparities in Internet penetration will narrow over time, but this is likely to be a long process. Qualitative differences with regard both to access and the creation of content are likely to persist as long as large income disparities remain, both among and within countries.

Libraries and other cultural organisations are responding both to globalization and the unevenness of globalization using a variety of strategies. The most obvious is to tailor services and the presentation of content to global as opposed to just local or national audiences. Such strategies may involve using

---

[2] Internet World Stats, March 31, 2009: <http://www.internetworldstats.com/stats.htm>

multilingual web presentations, and selecting for presentation on the web content likely to be of interest to international audiences. Libraries generally do not have an explicit mandate from their parent organisations or political masters to undertake efforts to bridge the international digital divide (they may have more of a mandate in the domestic context), but many are nonetheless active in this area. One of the strategies adopted is to partner with organisations that do have such a mandate, e.g., IFLA, UNESCO, and various private foundations.

DIVERSITY OF WAYS TO ACCESS DIGITAL CONTENT

A fourth condition that defines the current digital environment is the increasing diversity of ways to access digital content. This is true with regard to both devices and applications. Devices include traditional PCs, laptops, netbooks, iPods, mobile phones, personal digital assistants (PDAs), and e-book readers. Applications include traditional web pages, Web 2.0 applications, and social networking sites. Devices and applications are used in all kinds of combinations, producing both complexity and new opportunities to disseminate and access information.

Libraries are responding to this evolving environment by going to where the users are – making the content available where it will be found and used, for example Flickr, YouTube, and iTunes.

FROM TEXT TO AUDIO AND AUDIO-VISUAL MEDIA

A fifth aspect of today's digital environment is the relative shift from text to audio and audio-visual media. The amount of text-based content on the web continues to increase, but the more rapid growth has been in audio and audio-visual material. Indications of this trend, which is likely only to accelerate with technical and infrastructure improvements in streaming and broadband, include the spectacular success of YouTube and iTunes, and the fact that even traditional, text-dominated web sites (e.g., BBC, Reuters, *New York Times*) now offer a mix of text with audio and audio-visual resources.

Libraries and librarians may deplore the implications of this trend, which could suggest a decline in reading and an overall lowering of the level of literacy (as traditionally defined) in society. But libraries are coming up with strategies to respond to the trend. One is to exploit their own vast archival holdings of audio and audio-visual content by putting more such content on the web. Another is to provide mixed media treatments of themes and topics that previously might only have been presented through text and other visual materials.

Libraries and dedicated audio and audio-visual archives also have a special role in the preservation of these materials, which many of them are highlighting.

DOMINANT ROLE OF SEARCH ENGINES

A sixth general feature of the current digital environment is the dominant role of the search engines, Google in particular. Upwards of 70-80 percent of "up-stream" traffic to even very large and well-known sites can now come from search engine results, rather than from bookmarks, the keying in of URLs, or links from other web sites.

Search engines provide enormous benefits to users by offering rapid access to vast amounts of information in a way that would have been unthinkable a decade or two ago. Near-exclusive reliance on search engines does have poten-tial drawbacks, however. They include a possible tendency to fragment and disaggregate information and to change (for the worse) how people use and process information.[3] They also displace the use of other methods of finding information, e.g., online catalogues based on traditional metadata, which may be superior for many purposes. Not least, search engines have great potential for commercial and political manipulation, which inevitably creates nervous-ness among traditional librarians and many others about society's increasing reliance on them for access to information.

Whatever the potential drawbacks, libraries have no choice but to respond to the dominance of the search engines. Strategies that libraries are following in-clude exposing their traditional metadata, factoring external search into the de-sign of websites and digital libraries, sharing content so that it is located in and can be found in multiple places, and providing intellectual value-added *beyond* search as a way of attracting users who might be looking for something better or different.

EVER-RISING USER EXPECTATIONS

A final characteristic of the current digital environment, one that in a sense pervades all the others, is that of ever-rising user expectations. These expecta-tions operate in four areas: availability of content; findability of content; shar-ing and re-use of content and participation in content creation; and understand-ing content.

Users increasingly assume that everything should be online. They also tend to believe that everything should be free – a factor in the failure of numerous projects and ventures based on subscription or pay-per-view models (although

---

[3]   Prompting articles such as "Is Google killing general knowledge?" *Intelligent Life*, summer 2009.

this situation may be changing with the seeming revival of interest in fee-based models, e.g., Kindle, iTunes, certain newspapers that are starting to charge for previously free content).

Users increasingly expect that they should be able to search everything (both on the web as a whole and within large individual web sites) in a simple way and get rapid results and that they should have access to deep web content through search engines. They also want to be able to manipulate search results (through browsing, faceted searches), and they want suggestions based on such criteria as related information, user recommendations, popularity rankings, and so forth.

Users increasingly expect that they should be able to download, embed, link to, or email any piece of content. They also should have the opportunity to improve or transform content through corrections, tagging, translation and so forth. Users also want to be able to share content in social networks and to form virtual communities around content.

The fourth area in which ever-rising expectations apply is in that of understanding content. Users do not always "know what they are missing", but they do know when they are being overwhelmed by large amounts of content that they have difficulty in evaluating and prioritizing. Users tend to welcome selection and authentication by curators and experts, analysis and interpretation by experts, and features such as maps, timelines, visualisations, and interactives that make accessing content fun.

In all of these areas (except possibly the last), rising user expectations are the product of improved technology and innovations by commercial firms that have conditioned users to expect more, newer, and better applications and content. The fourth area – understanding – may be a bit different, as it is one in which libraries have certain comparative advantages and can shape user expectations.

Libraries and other cultural institutions are scrambling to adopt strategies to respond to this world of rising expectations. Such strategies include:

- increased efforts to find out what users are thinking and doing (e.g., usage statistics and qualitative feedback mechanisms);
- multi-institution collaborations (as a way of lowering costs and sharing ideas and best practices);
- exploiting the possibilities of open source;
- improving the design and functionality of sites;
- undertaking pilot projects to get user feedback and enable course corrections before large projects are launched;
- offering better search features;
- offering Web 2.0 features; and
- involving curators and outside experts to a greater degree than previously in digital library projects.

THE WORLD DIGITAL LIBRARY

The World Digital Library (WDL) was launched by the Library of Congress in 2005, at a time when the outlines of the digital environment as described above were already apparent. The WDL thus represents an example of a particular project that employs many of the strategies outlined above to respond to the digital challenge.

KEY FEATURES

Collaboration and Sharing with Partners. Initiated in cooperation with UNESCO, the WDL was planned as an inherently collaborative project. At the launch on April 21, 2009, the WDL had 34 partners in 21 countries. In the period since the launch, many more partners from many other countries have joined. A long term goal is to include at least one partner able to provide suitable content from each UNESCO member country.

Capacity-building in the Developing World. To enable libraries in the developing world to participate, the WDL seeks to build capacity in these institutions through the provision of training and equipment. During the 2006–2009 start up phase the WDL project set up two state-of-the-art digital conversion operations at partner institutions: at the National Library of Egypt, which has digitised scientific manuscripts for inclusion in the WDL, and at the Iraqi National Library and Archives, which has begun digitising at-risk magazines and newspapers from Iraq in 1860–1940 for inclusion in the WDL. An additional digital conversion centre is planned for the National Library of Uganda under a grant from the Carnegie Corporation of New York. Additional centres will be set up as funds become available.

Emphasis on Quality, Performance, and Metrics. The WDL development team started from an assumption that users are turned off by slow, clunky web sites. The WDL thus was optimized for speed and performance. Arrangements also were made to gather detailed user statistics following the public launch of the WDL in April 2009. These statistics, in conjunction with more qualitative feedback (user comments) will help in making ongoing performance improvements.

Consistent Metadata to Facilitate Search and Browse. Every item in the WDL is catalogued for place, time, topic, type of item, and contributing institution, as well as for language. This allows for consistent cross-temporal and cross-national searching. It ensures that what users find on the WDL is in response to what they are looking for and not an artefact of the quality or completeness of the bibliographic records.

Items Individually Indexable by Search Engines. The WDL metadata is exposed to the search engines in a way that enables users to find or be directed to individual WDL library items.

Multilingualism. The WDL interface functions in seven languages: Arabic, Chinese, English, French, Portuguese, Russian, and Spanish. Every item-level display, description, curator video, and navigational feature on the WDL is in these languages. At any point, users may switch to any other interface language. The content on the WDL is also linguistically diverse. More than forty languages are represented. Content in other languages will be added as the project develops and new partners join.

Options to Print, Download, Share, and Reuse Content. WDL users are offered, at the item-display level, several dozen options for what they can do with the WDL content. These options range from simple printing and e-mailing to sharing on Facebook and Twitter to distribution through more esoteric applications. Inclusion of these features in the WDL ensures that its content will be shared and re-purposed in ways that users increasingly demand and expect.

Features to Facilitate Understanding the Content. Features of the WDL intended to facilitate better understanding of the content include high quality metadata, item-level descriptions for every item, curator videos that explain particular items or collections, timelines, geographic clusters, and superior viewing technology.

Inclusion of Audio and Audio-Visual Content as Well as Text. The WDL includes historic audio and audio-visual content. Examples of audio content include a slave narrative from the Library of Congress and the earliest recording of the *Marseillaise* from the Bibliothèque nationale de France. Audio-visual content includes early films by the Lumière Brothers and Thomas Edison from the collections of the Library of Congress. Curator videos also form part of the audio-visual material on the WDL.

Reliance on Private Funding Sources. The WDL is funded by private sources. Major contributors to the project have included Google, Inc., the Qatar Foundation, the Carnegie Corporation of New York, the King Abdullah University of Science and Technology, Saudi Arabia, and Microsoft, Inc.

FUTURE PRIORITIES

The future priorities of the WDL are to continue implementing many of the strategies outlined above, adjusting where necessary in response to changing user demands and expectations. Near- and medium-term priorities include:

- Adoption of a WDL Charter;
- Development of online content transfer, cataloguing, and translation tools;
- Improved optimization for low bandwidth users;
- Development of applications for mobile devices;
- Establishment of a WDL blog to facilitate the sharing of user feedback and the discussion of content and technical issues;
- Conducting pilot projects with user communities to assist with translation.

DIGITAL LIBRARY FUTURES:
PRESSURES ON THE PUBLISHER-LIBRARIAN
RELATION IN THE ERA OF DIGITAL CHANGE

Herman P. Spruijt

ABSTRACT

The International Publishers Association (IPA) and IFLA have been in dialogue with each other through the IFLA IPA Working Group for many years. In this presentation IPA President Herman P. Spruijt shows how convergence in the digital area is also present in the dialogue between publishers and libraries, touching upon topics such as digital services, virtual libraries, e-publishing, Google and open access.

INTRODUCTION

The International Publishers Association (IPA)[1] is an international federation of national publishers associations representing book and journal publishing, based in Geneva. IPA's mission is to promote and protect copyright and to raise awareness for publishing as a force for economic, cultural and political development.

When talking about institutional strategies for the digital future: publishers still believe that quality content is crucial, but that the manifestation of the delivery (shape, form, place, context, links) to the end user will be the challenge for the coming years. Not as a push (publishers broadcasting), but as a pull with the end user "in the driver's seat".

We further believe strongly that we as publishers need the assistance of the library community: the so called convergence between strategic partners.

I have spent my whole active working life in book and journal publishing. Much of that time was spent talking to and working with librarians, notably as one of the founders (and co-chair) of our joint IFLA IPA Working Group. The idea behind establishing this joint working group goes back to 1998 when the Executive Committee of IPA (under the Presidency of Alain Grund) met in Paris with at that time the President of IFLA, Madame Christine Deschamps.

These were turbulent times when both publishers and librarians experienced in their day to day life the first introductions of on-line products, and we were

---

[1]   <http://www.internationalpublishers.org/>

both trying to find out whether or not our relations could be the same as they were in the past. Subjects like licensing, copyright and its exceptions in a digital world divided our constituencies. In addition, the notion of "users' rights" and "the debate surrounding journal pricing" created a seemingly unbridgeable divide between libraries and publishers.

However, by identifying issues of common interest the members of the IFLA IPA Working Group have been engaged in a series of very interesting and useful dialogues with, at the librarian's side as co-chair, Ingrid Parent and Claudia Lux respectively. No issue has been spared, and discussions have been loud, sometimes even slightly aggressive (at our side), emotional (at your side) and controversial, but we have discovered that even in the areas of greatest controversy there is more that publishers and librarians have in common than that divides us.

CONTROVERSY BUT STILL GOOD RELATIONS

We have been "fighting" many times in the last decades, and believe it or not, there were at that time even ideas about the disintermediation of the library and of the publisher. There were both publishers and librarians who thought they could finally take on the other's role. Would not all the advantages of the internet and the local area networks on the campuses, allow direct access to the desktops of the students and researchers? In other words: why do you need a library if the publisher could provide direct access to users? Today some recent developments seem to confirm these ideas. Some publishers are now offering subscriptions that are the equivalent of access to a virtual library. The digital revolution has moved from e-journals to e-books, which are being offered in bulk deals just like journals.

And could libraries not become themselves the publishers? Equally some libraries have become the owners or partners of digital repositories and these repositories have the potential of becoming dynamic databases in their own right. Like for example Europeana, where libraries supply their content to what "in the past" would have required publisher's involvement (such as the *Encyclopedia Britannica*).

Such convergence isn't necessarily new. Librarians have traditionally been on the boards of university presses. In recent times library and university publishing arms have been moved together. MIT[2] made a start a number of years ago. Since then Penn State, New York University and others have moved these parts of their organisation together.

---

[2]   <http://web.mit.edu/>

TOWARDS GLOBAL DIGITAL LIBRARIES?

It is important to consider, however, the context that the globalization of the internet now allows some libraries to provide such excellent digital services, that they are serving clients outside their own community. It is nothing special to hear a scientist explain that he/she no longer uses only his/her own university library but also has seamless online access to all the content needed from foreign libraries. That is what we call: user driven, de-coupled from the traditional information base: her or his local library.From there, it is only a small step from national cooperation and file/document sharing between academic libraries to a global marketplace for virtual libraries, in which libraries, just like publishers, compete on a global scale for the attention of the readers.

Just another example to show the ease of globalization for both the rights owner and content user in the field of rights clearance: The American Copyright Clearance Centre (CCC) has developed business- and service models that follow their vision of becoming "the global hub for rights clearance": a fast, easy and intuitive global web based (micro) payment system with many front end features. This will help all rights holders (authors and publishers) to deal with their IP centrally and with consistent policies all over the world. More importantly in this context it allows the individual user to obtain any document easily, without institutional hassle 24/7. This can in part replace the certainly not user friendly current system of collecting societies with their largely national solutions which transfer the monies from country to country, taking 'their fair share' and distributing revenues on spurious metrics rather than actual usage: a burden for content owners and users alike.

So, what we see here is that publishers, libraries and collecting societies follow their patrons or customers into the digitally borderless world, and we only then discover how our international partnerships relied on an assumption that we do not compete on the same ground but complement each other.

CLOSER COOPERATION

Rather than replacement, we find ourselves in a situation of increasing entanglement, so much so that it is becoming hard for outsiders to distinguish where one's task begins and the other party's ends. Archiving and preservation used to be the role of libraries. With the digital subscription model it has moved to the publisher. But at the same time, because of the dynamic and ever-changing databases, archiving and service and "solution" providing, move closer together. Elsevier, a large science publisher, now backs up a number of its servers in the Royal Library of the Netherlands as well as through the library-supported Portico and CLOCKSS programmes.

The change that comes with digital technologies means that e-publishing the process no longer ends with the sale to the library of a physical issue, book or even a license, let alone the journal subscription. With backward and forward linking "on the fly", journals are now dynamic databases with a significant amount of daily updates. Where this storage and "archiving" was the role of the library it is now almost impossible for a library to host these dynamic databases on site. They are now the responsibility of the publisher and the linking to other publishers databases is organised through metadata by pre-competitive standards agencies like Crossref ®[3] and because of the technology used, no longer in the domain of librarians.

A NEW PLAYER WHICH SETS ITS OWN RULES...

Whilst we were squabbling, Google was founded and began to pursue its mission to organise the world's information and make it universally accessible and useful. And Google *has* of course created a vast content database that is de facto very difficult to match by any individual library or any single publisher because of its clearer views of aggregation. What libraries could not do because of money and copyright laws Google did.

So, is Google a threat to libraries and publishers?[4] I understand that the debate is raging among librarians. Is Google the first commercial partner that shares the values of the library community, or is it the final commercial partner that will gradually make libraries and librarians superfluous? The same questions arise for publishers: is Google there to help market our books or replace us?

The danger of Google is that all its strength is built on a specific business model that is extremely clever, but nonetheless parasitical.[5] As an editor of the Wall Street Journal noted, it needs content, verified quality content with authority, but it will not pay for it.

Google relies on access to virtually all content for free. This puts Google in a huge and singular competitive advantage because it has far greater resources to discover and to unlock new content sources than any of its competitors, public (the library) or private (the publisher).

Clever cooperation with a series of libraries, spread around the world, means that Google will provide faster access to more content, selling it back into the libraries, competing with the shrinking library budgets, leading us to ask "for free" at what a price in the end?

---

[3]   See < http://www.crossref.org/>

[4]   Today, business sectors that consider Google to be an actual or potential competitor include advertising, financial services, TV networks, telephone companies, Internet retailers and software houses. It also includes publishers and libraries: <http://www.strategy-business.com/media/file/sb49_07404.pdf>

[5]   <http://www.theaustralian.news.com.au/business/story/0,28124,25293711-7582,00.html >

QUALITY SEARCH WITH THE END-USER IN MIND?

And what about quality, and especially quality the end user expects from libraries? Does Google really deliver what the end-user requires and expects? The Google library project started in Academic Research Libraries. Are their end-users -researchers and scientists- waiting for the rough content (without illustrations, graphs, etc) and rough search algorithms Google delivers?

We heard today: users look at the first 25 hits and trust that the search engine made the right selection. Were the libraries considering this trust, bestowed on their shoulders or did they only want to make their content available in digital format, ripe and green? Is the size of the corpus really so important to sacrifice the quality of the displayed content and the search?

The publishing community is flabbergasted: honestly, publishers like me are really puzzled and certainly do not recognize these decisions at all from all our "quality of content" discussions over the years with the same librarians who signed these contracts with Google. Some of the same libraries participated in many of the user behavior studies between publishers and libraries, staring with programmes like Tulip[6] and stressed the need for efficiency and quality of the search results. So, what went wrong? What went wrong in our relation to sincerely serve the end-user at the best of our knowledge and possibilities?

ADDING VALUE AROUND THE DIGITAL COPY

Beside the serious concerns we have as publishers about the legality of those libraries who agreed to cooperate with Google, we cannot fully understand why this form of "sale" of content, acquired over so many decades and sometimes centuries, with Government money (!) is digitised at such a poor quality (rush-rush) just because the libraries involved would receive a "free digital copy" (wow!) of their holdings! Why were those libraries not prepared to lobby with their publishers for solid solutions financed by their governments and Science Foundations and support the publishers, who are still digitizing at high quality levels (PDF, XML with proper metadata) their backlists, first in journals and now in books?

Both IPA and IFLA have committed themselves (and especially Claudia Lux, IFLA President 2007–2009) to lobby governments to support the digitisation of our library heritage. Publishers like Oxford University Press, Wiley, the American Chemical Society, WoltersKluwer, Springer and Elsevier have invested since the early nineties in the quality of their products; specifically dedicated to the wishes of end-users (scholars and scientists) than any generic

---

[6]   Karen Hunter (ed) (1996), Tulip final report , Amsterdam, Elsevier Science ISBN 0-444-82540-1

Google or other search engine can and will offer. McGraw Hill, Springer and even smaller publishers like Brill, Cambridge University Press and Oxford University Press are now investing and have invested heavily in book databases which are so superior in quality, searchability and dedication to the specific wishes of their respective users that it pays off to pay for these products.

Let's be fair: can society rely on Google Book Search algorithms as the only guides through the jungle of published information? Are the amount of quality hits in Wiley InterScience, Springer Link and Science Direct and the like not far better than any Google outcome?

And what about all the projects and investments at the library side? The access-projects of the British Library; the archiving investments of the Dutch Royal Library and the ongoing investments in content and accessibility of OCLC. They cannot be matched by Google products now and in the near future, and why then support these as professionals? Only because they are "for free"?

And let's not forget the result of all the digitisation of archives and repositories, supported by publishers and libraries, for the activities of J-store and other "aggregators", with the consent of the rights holders (yes, sometimes difficult negotiations, but in almost all cases eventually with mutual consent). Will they not pay off in the end? Why did we both support these activities, projects and investments? Because they all have the end-user in mind and take her/him seriously! So, why that impatience? As said before: time and again we, publishers and librarians, are thrown into each others arms: let's make it work together with our proven skills and proven commitment!

OPEN ACCESS: AN ULTIMATE SOLUTION?

The last subject I would like to only touch upon is open access. Not as a possible business model, but because the full implementation might allow new players to enter our world again with challenging business models and sharp pricing, again, not necessarily prepared to pay for the content itself.
We see this (content for "free") trend in different forms of publishing coming up again strongly. It is not the user who pays but someone else in the chain, be it advertiser or originator, supporter or funding agency.

The Joint Statement by the IFLA-IPA Working Group symbolizes the new state of debate that we are in today. We have enough experience to move from opinion based politics to fact based policies. Sweeping generalizations are making way for a differentiated approach. We are now doing some proper research together (see the Peer Project with the emphasis on user and user research).[7] No business model is being ruled out, and no single business model

---

[7]   <http://www.peerproject.eu>

should be imposed irrespective of its impact on that particular area of research, because we know that the Internet develops too quickly and in too unpredictable directions to force the will of any particular interest group onto its workings. We also know, however, that in order to see what will work we must try out new options. A lot of publishers, commercial and not-for-profit, have their "open access"- publishing policies in place, and we now wait and see how this idea will be taken up by the scholarly community.

Why this dwelling on open access on a symposium on user behavior? Because it has everything to do with securing usage of the published content, and a fair access of any author to the system, poor or rich, irrespectively whether she/he or her/his institution can afford to pay the "entrance bill". Eventually any other business model should at least increase the usage of content. It looks to me as if what used to be a fight of tug-of-war between publishers and libraries is turning into more of a dance. We are twirling around each other, getting closer as the world is turning faster around us. We are still stepping on each other's toes, occasionally, as we are learning this new dance.

REINVENTING CENTURIES-OLD RELATIONS AGAIN!

Let's go back to the discussion of the scientist/researcher, who did not fall back on her/his own library alone (anymore), combined with the global solutions CCC-type of organisations offer for access and rights clearance. This is just an example of our changing world; indeed why should a user just use her/his own local library service in a virtual world?

The changing publisher-librarian relation, be it dancing or fighting, can easily become under fierce attack again by an outsider as a new player. Like all Internet technology companies, Google was able to smash into our world, because they had a great technological solution for a single core element of our work. But the tasks of librarians and publishers are more complex and more sophisticated. This is both our weakness and our strength.

As I said, this is not the end. New players will stand up and will be able to change the scene in a very short period again. With the virtualisation of existing brick and mortar relations and increased competition, together with the ease of acquiring and aggregating content (almost for free, certainly if open access gets ground under its feet), it is not unthinkable but almost likely that a new superior global and virtual service may be on offer elsewhere soon.

And let's be fair again; while we were quarreling about rights and the library's lack of funding for digitisation,[8] Google was able to access "our world"

---

[8]   Google appears to be speaking with the Library of Alexandria to digitise all works (many of those obtained as gifts from publishers at the opening), with a special interest in the Arab language titles; in addition, the French National Library (BNF) is, according to Mr Denis Bruck-

because millions of orphan works were waiting to be digitised, and because they could smash and pay their way through the legitimate concerns that publishers and libraries had with such bold commercial digitisation project.

But there is not only gloom and doom. We can read this week in the press about the re-launch of three e-book readers (Sony Reader, Amazon's Kindle[9] and Borders iLiad)[10] and Google seems to play a positive role by providing works out of copyright to them. Assuming that the rights will be cleared by the suppliers this really is a breakthrough and helps to develop the book market and test the market.

CONCLUSIONS

I like to urge our two professions to explore new ways of collaboration as public-private partnerships which are not only based on a commercial relationship (of sellers and buyers), but on our mutual interest to serve our readers.

The debate surrounding Google has highlighted our joint weaknesses, in particular the lack of funding for digitisation and the slow progress of our complicated relationships to create good solutions.

By focusing on our weaknesses, we have forgotten our strengths. In recognizing strengths, libraries should stop seeing themselves as victims of the publishing market, but as partners that have more to bring to the table than the far too meagre library budgets. It is only when libraries bring their knowledge about their users that publishers can develop products that serve these users best.

It is still my conviction that together, libraries and publishers can provide an excellent service to the people and the public interests that we both serve: our users, our readers.

---

mann, negotiating with Google to digitise its holdings, because there are no funds available from the French Government (NRC-Handelsblad 20-08-2009)

[9] In : Financial Times, August 26 2009

[10] iRex Technologies [info@irextechnologies.com]

CLOSING SESSION

CLOSING ADDRESS

Penny Carnaby

I would like to start by acknowledging all the people who have put today to-gether. It was a brave agenda. The Ministry of Cultural and Heritage, the IFLA Professional Committee, and the University, we are really grateful to you, be-cause this is an a-typical thing to do for IFLA. And I for one have learned a huge amount today.

What I will do in trying to summarise all the wonderful things people have said today, is to give you an overview, but also share with you some of the things that I was thinking about personally during the day. I am reasonably op-timistic about our position, but I have to say that I did lurch into some feelings of extreme discomfort at times, and probably amounted to something like ter-ror, when I thought: "Actually, how do you bring all of this stuff together?"

In my summary I will bring up things that are comfortable for all of us, but also things that are not so comfortable.

THE CONTEXT

Let's first focus on the context. When we talk about digital age and digital paradigm, we have to realize we are literally talking about a new age, not just about a new generation. And this new age may be as significant as the industrial age. It is really challenging us in ways that has never been the case before. The fundamental context of today has been more around what we are seeing as a changing pattern in the creation of knowledge. And the reason I say that, is that most of us present in this room have been used to the authoritative authenti-cated tome of knowledge that is so typical of the institutions we work for.

That's changing as we are really challenged by the "informal" knowledge systems. A new equity is emerging that puts citizen-created content on central stage. It gets us to ask questions that are very uncomfortable for us, and which have emerged during the day. "Is citizen-created content, which is sometimes anarchic, unpredictable, and not authoritative, any less worthy in terms of the formal knowledge systems that we've been so used to? "I am going to keep that idea as the context for the summary of the day. So let's launch in.

THE USER TAKING CENTRE STAGE

Clearly, the star of this morning was the user taking centre stage. And quite rightly, we had a lot of very thoughtful comments. David Nicholas, for example,

took us through the new generation of user behaviour in the virtual environment. Yes, he did say: "The future is now." And I was sitting back, thinking:
"Well, yes, yes, I know that, but that is the younger generation, the generation
X." And then I thought he was really unkind to all of us, because he said that we
are all the Google generation. This meant that I actually had to engage, and that
it concerned not only "all the kids around us". That was a very useful insight.

Then he drew us into the changing patterns of how people read, and how
they search for information. He did tell us something that a lot of the women in
the room know already. We know, David that men shop around more in their
seeking behaviours. The presentation of David Nicholas really was a very good
start of the day.

It was followed really well by Daniel (Teruggi) talking about the Europeana
user perspective. And I just had the sense, listening to that, that it was an in-
tensely respectful approach to trying to understand what the user's perspective
was. Teruggi worked through a lot of personas in an attempt to understand
what the user experience would be. He talked about multi-faceted personalities,
and non-functional as well as functional specifications. And then he talked
about the user I had not really thought about at all, and I feel terribly guilty, the
robots – in fact, the biggest user of all. We have to have a big rethink about
robots.

The third session was taken care of by Elke (Greifeneder). How many of
you felt deeply ashamed that you might be in that 50 percent? I was feeling
quite comfortable for a while, representing a small national library. If we had
more money, we'd been doing decent user surveys. But this idea got blown out
of the water too, so I couldn't even rest on that. Greifeneder's presentation
brought a lot of thoughts about those user surveys, and it wasn't a great report
guide for us, to be honest. We simply don't have the capability.

"TRADE ME" – A WELLINGTON EXAMPLE

In New Zealand we have an addiction to "Trade me", a website where we buy
and sell and exchange. At the same time we rate the trustworthiness of people
covering things like how easy they were to work with. It occurred to me that
"Trade me" might be a better way of surveying how the user is experiencing
services and then we wouldn't have to delve into areas in which some of us
clearly are not all that competent. If there is one new way to survey, as
Greifeneder stated, "Trade me" was the one I thought about.

That whole focus of users in the first morning session was really good. Each
of the three speakers crafted a very interesting and different perspective.

What I'll do here is give you a bit of an idea of a user in Wellington, the
capital city of New Zealand. This is a New Zealand student that probably lives
200 meters up the road from our National Library building. And just in case

you think that New Zealand is the only country in the world to have students like the one you are about to hear, I suspect that it is either deeply depressing in terms of what she is about to say, or she is having a Tesco moment. And it may be that she doesn't know that she was accessing the gorgeous and wonderful collections of the National Library of New Zealand but anyway, here is what she got to say. It is deeply uncomfortable but I don't think I am the only one.

"I am a Wellington student. My school is literary two minutes away from here. They gave me a lovely assignment, on local history, and believe it or not, we did not come here (National Library of New Zealand). We just went straight to the computer, and I guess that that shows that our feelings on technology, we just even didn't think about it, we just went straight there. All the information that is available is here: the new stories, the articles, everything that was available on the net. I think this goes not only for students that are only 2 minutes away from the library, but for all students in the greater Wellington region, all over the North island, the South Island, the whole of New Zealand, everyone can easily access that information."

I am sure that you have students near you and that leads me to the sort of information she is seeking. And that leads nicely to a summary of the organisational response.

In this context, I imagined the user in Italy. And spontaneously, my thinking moved to the extraordinary networks and knowledge infrastructures that a lot of people here in the room today are creating. The information that is available at the international level and the organisational response to it, that is extraordinary. It raises as many challenges as it does opportunities. I really had a deeply subversive thought on this particularly.

The idea of the British Library subsidizing American scholars: think of all the information flowing around the world. It is absolutely true; the changing patterns of e-scholarship, of how ideas are generated, and no longer have the geographical or organisational boundaries. And it becomes very difficult with the funding models being still so strictly organisationally focused. There are some common ingredients of the new knowledge networks. We have for instance been talking about the library that never sleeps, the 24 by 7, the need to be accessible to users when, where and how they want it. I regard now the end user as the co-creator of new knowledge.

PARADIGMS OF POWER

Then we started to delve into that in the web 2 environment. And there are changing paradigms of power as well, which I find hugely exciting. These are very challenging concepts to all of us. There is a new equity emerging and it is challenging cultural institutions like our own to fundamentally rethink everything that we thought of safely.

Between Einar (Røttingen) and Susan (Hazan) they traversed the tensions of formal and informal knowledge systems. Who could fail to be moved by Røttingen's story of Grieg and the depth of musical scholarship that was unleashed by the website he discussed. I find that a fascinating story. This is where collaboration came up, which also had been a theme of the day. Røttingen talked about the collaboration of the researchers, the librarian, the technologists, and it was an extraordinary story that he told, that almost intimate relationship with each one of those music scores. It was also amazing to see technology, the computer programme, actually changing the key at the touch of a fingertip. It was fascinating. And just as I was getting into Grieg's piano concerto, I had some anxiety as I thought: "Oh no! Will we be super serving the super served? How much money we'll be spending, on one wonderful experience around music scholarship?"

Wouldn't it be better to unleash, liberate content and let the end user mash it up and engage with it? This idea brought up all sorts of tension, but then I calmed down and thought: "We need the deep and meaningful – the scholarship – and we need the massification – that's what citizens created." Susan Hazan demonstrated this tension very ably. She herself felt the tension of those uncomfortable questions, where she and her organisation were actually – in terms of description – not able to release that to folksonomies tagging. Remember her red line. That said a lot. We need to step over the line. And we find it so difficult. We are responding with our "old generation thinking" about "new generation knowledge systems" that could add so much richness and story to the things that have become quite traditional for us.

INFRASTUCTURES AND LAYERS

Then we moved into an incredibly interesting part of the day where two countries presented their inside stories. Professor Zhu and Rossella Caffo really talked about how China and Italy were looking at connecting their countries, for instance on how the union catalogues formed the connection of knowledge systems across their countries. And it brought another very uncomfortable question for us: there are so many infrastructures and layers. We have this huge national pride in creating our connections across our countries. But it does lead us to the question on how much we are keeping on repeating things? And how much have we been joining up and doing together? I think that is a very important question for us to be answering today.

BUSINESS MODELS AND GREAT CONVERSATIONS

The latter stage of the afternoon was taken by John (van Oudenaren) and Herman (Spruijt). Van Oudenaren challenged us to really think of distant business models, of different strategies. We talked through fundraising, the need to think in a more joined up, diverse way of accessing digital content, liberating content, open source, all of these things. We could spend whole days on some of these issues that have been raised today.

There is a bit of a debate that is well worth on picking here: Van Oudenaren said that the World Digital Library is facing the challenge of Google, with one of our true value propositions, which is Quality. This is an interesting topic to consider. Is quality, that deep research, the example of the great scores and librettos; is that the dividing space? Or is it something much more ubiquitous?

Herman Spruijt did some direct talking of those robust discussions between publishers and libraries. These are great conversations to have, and we must continue to have them. Spruijt talked about new partnering, new business models, and public private partnerships. We've got to find a way to work together with the publishing industries. It doesn't make sense for the library and information sector and publishing industry not to work together. But I expect there is a bit of give and take on both sides that is yet to be explored.

It was interesting that it took the end of the day for us to mention the G-word, since we could probably have talked about that all day too.

TENSIONS AND NON DISCUSSED TOPICS

In summary: Many topics have come through today. Quite appropriately, the user was centre stage, the star of the show, even if we came at it from many different ways.

Some topics didn't come up for me. I just want to work through some of those tensions, for you to think about. Tomorrow, CDNL, the Directors of national libraries will meet for the day, and we will talk about our vision for connecting the national libraries of the world through their digital collections. It is a really ambitious idea, but it foresees a system in a remote part of a country, like for example Argentina, to be able to explore and discuss and engage with the other digital collections in the world, with their owners and their users. And to achieve this, in a world that is sometimes divided by political, cultural, social and economic differences, it has got the potential to unite us in a really profound way.

It is not an issue around technology. It is really an issue around the following question: "Is this what libraries fundamentally are about? About the freedom of access to information and to knowledge. As places of discourse, argument and celebration of cultures". That is the more philosophical question that I pose.

The digital revolution has been and is, a great democratiser, but I have not heard much today about what we are doing with the emerging knowledge system, the informal knowledge system, the anarchic system of citizen-created content. One of the things that keep me awake at night is the "delete generation". Every minute, every hour, every second of every day in this world, we are deleting our memory, our heritage, our stories, and our sense of the knowledge of mankind. And I personally would put this issue on centre stage with the completely new taxonomies we're developing, to try and get our heads round the unacceptable loss of data, of knowledge in this digital age. I am particularly talking about the citizen-created content and we must ask ourselves the following question: "Is citizen-created content, which gets to us sometimes much faster, in a much more immediate way, any less worthy thinking about in terms of preservation? And if we delete this, are we deleting a whole part of our social history memory?" For me, that is the issue that wasn't covered today.

A CHALLENGE TO EACH ONE OF US

In closing up, and in final summary: what we have seen today is a challenge to each one of us. At the same time it is also a celebration of all the wonderful work that has been done internationally. There certainly are new challenges ahead, but what I heard today is a very thoughtful view both from the formal knowledge systems and from the user perspective, and a very respectful view of the understanding the end user. We need to continue looking for the opportunities to join up much more – in infrastructures, in projects – so that we can liberate knowledge systems of the world through the digital environment.

More content, more culture, more heritage. It is an enormous privilege, and at the same time an enormously challenging profession, that we are involved in. And I for one found the day very provocative. I hope you all have got something from it as well. Thank you for listening and together, we need to do a lot more joined up thinking.

FINAL SUMMARY

Anna Maria Tammaro

What is the future for digital libraries? Experts and speakers from various parts of the world who took part in the IFLA Conference expressed views based on their own experience, setting out various scenarios some of which were truly ground-breaking. At the end of the Conference, all those involved were aware that digital libraries are a firm reality and that the present situation is to dictate the outlook for the future.

This IFLA Conference focussed on the evolution of libraries into digital libraries: how can libraries be steered towards strategies that will equip them to offer innovative services that meet users' expectations? Something that we were certainly aware of by the end of the sessions was that there is an air of optimism where the future of the library is concerned. What has traditionally been seen as a collection of physical artefacts and a physical space has now been given new life with traditional services being combined with the technology required to enable access, undeniably taking on a whole new perspective. Susan Hazan presented a number of examples:

> "When the Library of Congress uploads 4,880 of its 14 million pictures to Flickr, UNESCO tries to fit the Memory of the World into its global library in order to guard against collective amnesia, and the New Bibliotheca Alexandrina becomes the home of the Wayback Machine, the mammoth Internet Archive that contains a snapshot of all web pages on every website since 1996, you know that it is time to rethink the term 'library' in a way that makes sense for the 21st Century."

These libraries have clearly shown that the introduction of digital resources into their collection and changes in the way their services are organised result in an increase in user numbers as well as a greater variety in the type of users. By way of a targeted application of digital technology, the library can realize its full potential, expanding on its facilities by offering services previously beyond reach. Rather than competing with the library as an institution, technology instead takes on the role of catalyst, helping them to improve the way they operate and to break new barriers, transforming them into virtual spaces in which the library becomes a centre for lifelong learning, a centre for society as a whole and a centre for participatory networks. But the application of technology alone is not sufficient to successfully embrace this development, given the challenges it presents; professionals have to manage the change and find creative solutions.

As many of the speakers at the conference emphasised, this change to libraries is not one having limited significance, nor is it merely an incidental change, such as moving over from paper files to digital. It is instead a change that goes to the very heart of the library as an institution, starting with the core of the library: the services that it provides.

THE LIBRARY TREE

The library in its current form can be compared to a tree reaching out to the sky. Just as a tree has roots, so does the library, in the essential role that it plays: assisting the user in accessing information. The library's roots are also found in the procedures and methods used to organise knowledge, as well as in the link that the library has with the past: over time, the libraries have employed the most efficient forms of technology to organise, manage, communicate and spread knowledge.

Just like a tree, the library has a solid trunk as it base, together with its branches. The trunk is the library as an institution and its strategies. Some libraries are centuries old; others have a shorter history. But the library as an institution continues to be an essential base for the continuation of the services provided and their sustainability over time, starting with one of the most important services: guaranteeing permanent access to the collection. Typical features of the library as an institution are the organisation of knowledge in the best possible way and the management of financial and human resources, the library being an organisation providing a service to society: guaranteed free access to information.

A huge mass of leaves make up the foliage of the tree, representing the information resources and the access permitted to the user; the richer and more lush the foliage, the more effective the service granting access. The digital library service is an extensive one across the board, with libraries not only able to help users by accessing resources located elsewhere but also providing new means of access, by way of the remote user, being someone who never in fact visits the library.

But this extension in the access services provided by the library can function only if planned correctly. David Nicholas, one of the experts at the IFLA Conference, gave this warning:

"Libraries are still working on the basis of the old paradigm – there is a risk of decoupling".

The risk that many libraries run when converting to digital is that of simply creating their double, with the organisation of their resources and services being a carbon copy of the original.

In her presentation analyzing the various evaluation methods used by digital libraries, Elke Greifeneder was another speaker at the IFLA Conference to point out that:

> "We see a mismatch between what we are analyzing now and what should be analyzing."

She was also commenting:

> "How can we be aware of users needs? Now it is done according to libraries preferences".

So what form should the new service model take on? Rather than hiding resources from users in the "deep web" or making access for the user difficult with obstacles such as authorisation to overcome, digital resources and the digital library's services need to be brought into the user's home.

We need to find a way of making the resources more accessible at large. Susan Hazan posed the following question:

> "Libraries as a place and/or a virtual space? How can we create a community?"

And David Nicholas also flagged up the following:

> "Do users have the necessary skills?"

About the user: Daniel Teruggi claims that we need to focus on information behaviour and interface design. The library user is changing, and libraries have to embrace these changes. The library that fails to do so runs a huge risk: withering and becoming a dry and dusty museum, it can lose out on its role to the advantage of its competitors. Libraries cannot and must not distance themselves from their users.

But what direction is our user taking? In search of information, the user is increasingly going on the net, rather than going to the library. But information is now retrieved in a different way. Research that merits careful consideration is that carried out by London University College research institute CIBER into user research behaviour on the Internet. CIBER's research was based on the analysis of logs collected over a seven year period and studied the type of pages looked at and at research styles. David Nicholas described the new information research behaviour being seen:

> "Information seeking is frenetic: bouncing, navigating, checking and viewing!"

And:

"Surprisingly, it is not centred on viewing the full text document".

This is particularly apparent where the new generation of users is concerned. Many teens today who use the Internet are actively involved in participatory cultures, joining online communities (Facebook, message boards, game clans), producing creative work in new formats (digital sampling, modding, fan video making, fan fiction), working in teams to complete tasks and develop new knowledge (such as Wikipedia), and shaping the flow of media (as in blogging or podcasting).

And what on the quality of the resources? The choice of information remains the privilege of libraries that filter and organise their collections. To what extent is any evaluation carried out regarding the performance of this quality filter? To a limited extent, in David Nicholas's view:

"There is noise and overload of information: BUT this is the price to be paid!!!"

Those creating digital content have multiplied in number and are no longer simply publishers. Susan Hazan described the huge rich market of information producers and information providers. Roles are often confused and also compete with one another; libraries, in their mass digitisation programmes, often take on the role of content creator, and publishers supplying access to their digital collections seek to take on the role of intermediary. Those new to the business, such as search engines, with Google being one example, have graduated from their initial role of supplying access to content produced by others, to starting to build digital content collections.

Finally, and this is perhaps the most important development of all, users themselves have become content creators. On the subject of music scholars, Einar Røttingen focused on "user cooperation" in the creation of digital content. What changes are there in this new role that users have taken on?

"They will also become producers."

And:

"They can create metadata."

The increase in the number of content creators and providers of services has a considerable impact on digital libraries. The distinction between content creator and provider of services is not an easy one to make. Similarly, two digital library scenarios have been clearly marked out: the first follows the more technical paradigm of digital creation; the second is more oriented towards services and participatory networks.

The first paradigm is illustrated by what would seem to be one of the more widespread tendencies of digital libraries that have developed out of libraries that digitizing their bibliographic collections, following a service model that can be described as Digitise – Archive – Distribute: the archival scenario.

With this model, professionals should return to collection development, leaving resource discovery to the search engine. Nevertheless, there exists another service model, one that was illustrated by the speakers during the course of the IFLA Conference and being the reference service model in the digital sphere, with active support for the user in order to access knowledge, offering what the consumers want, without spending time and money on the wrong things.

In the Access to Knowledge scenario, we see the librarian as facilitator, extending its role to the use and the sharing of resources, in competition with, or in synergy with, others in the information market. As David Nicholas pointed out, an economic model exists in support of this model. The value of the work done by digital libraries can be quantified and above all appreciated by the individual user and by the community. "Professionals' need to be 'smart shoppers' who play the market".

With regard to the setting up of either of the two service scenarios, various strategies were suggested: working towards the usability of the interfaces that build the library's virtual space, encouraging the convergence and cooperation of institutions of cultural importance such as libraries, archives and museums and launching new partnerships with all those interested in the information market.

USABILITY

There is an important link to be found in the new services made available by libraries using the internet and technology. The first reaction to the challenge· of reaching users using the Internet to get the information they want has, for the libraries, been to set up the virtual access space on the internet, known as the "portal".

Picking up the metaphor of the tree again, the portal can be seen as the tree's foliage. This now stretches as far as the end user, reaching out to a user that is remote, and holding itself out as a preferred point of access to information, together with or in competition with search engines.

Based on his experience of the Europeana digital library and his experience with audiovisuals and multimedia documents, Daniel Teruggi, Head of Research Institute INA highlighted the advantages of and the problems encountered in the usability of portals. At its simplest, the term "usable" means "can be used". The portals are tools that enable access to be personalised, resolving the problem of information overload and the problem of a lack of quality information. The advantages of the portals can also be found in the opportunity to bring various collections together such as archives, libraries and museums, with the same interface. This opportunity encourages the convergence of cultural institutions, resulting in considerable advantages for users. Usability was defined by Daniel Teruggi as:

"The ease with which people can employ a tool or object in order to achieve a particular goal."

From the point of view of technology, where Human-Computer Reaction (HCI) is concerned, usability can mean a range of things, including:

– How efficiently and effectively users can achieve their goals with a system;
– How easily users can learn to use the system ("learnability");
– How well the system helps the user avoid making errors, or recover from errors;
– The quality of the user experience – whether users enjoy working with the system, or whether they find it frustrating;
– How well the system fits into the context in which it is used.

Problems with usability of the interface are linked to human-computer interaction but are technological only in part.

Which model should be sought in designing the portals? Not the library catalogue model, but the Google or Wikipedia model. The view expressed by Daniel Teruggi is that there are a certain number of considerations as regards usability when designing a tool, software or a website:

– Who are the users?
– What do they want or need?
– Which is the use context?
– What is their background?

Teruggi concluded that users need to be involved in the design of the interface, with an Advisory Board being set up, comprising group of users interested in the portal and keen to discuss or take part in evaluation studies (currently this is under construction by Europeana).

THE INTERNATIONAL COMMUNITY

The digital library has to opt for the strategy of cooperation. The choice of such a strategy, one that has been successfully adopted and followed by libraries for years, would now seem to be an essential one. Every digital library is part of an international community of digital libraries, and searches of this international community in its entirety can be done on line, with full access via portals, such as the Europeana portal, or by digital content aggregators or by search engines.

Whilst a full search online is possible, cooperation on the part of libraries nevertheless calls for central coordination and political encouragement both from the point of view of necessary funding and also to avoid certain problems arising such as unnecessary duplication of the digitization of certain items. All the cooperative initiatives by digital libraries share a distributed approach, with coordination structures at local, regional and national level, and close liaison with national digitization strategies and the active participation of thousands of cultural institutions on every level and in every sector. Rossella Caffo (ICCU) and Zhu Qiang (Beijing University Library) and John Van Oudenaeren (UNESCO) set out how to coordinate digital libraries, putting forward solutions for problems of an organisational, financial and legal nature.

But cooperation is not limited to digital libraries. It is now "cross domain". Digital convergence has also prompted convergence on an organisational and cultural level on the part of cultural institutions as a whole. Ingrid Parent (IFLA President-elect) has declared that libraries, archives, and museums have evolved along separate paths for very good reasons, but the information age that we are now in, involving new information and communications technology, draws them together as never before. The IFLA, together with the International Council on Archives (ICA), the International Council of Museums (ICOM), the International Council on Monuments and Sites (ICOMOS) and the Coordinating Council of Audiovisual Archives Associations (CCAAA) have a longstanding relationship based on cooperation, and have now agreed to focus even further on the opportunities for cooperation where libraries, archives and museums have mutual interests and operate in similar fields.

Library, Archive and Museum (LAM) convergence is based on digital resources, with the exchange of, for example, raw data, standards and formats, learning resources, materials. The preservation and upkeep of digital collection represent a perfect example of an area in which libraries, archives and museums can profitably work together. But LAM convergence is capable of going well beyond putting together a shared collection. There is much to be done to facilitate access to digital libraries, using integrated services tailored for different user communities.

NEW PARTNERSHIP

A different approach to the management of digital libraries means a new entrepreneurial spirit, involving new partnerships with publishers, commercial information services and organisations in the public and private sector. These partnerships go beyond the traditional relationships with library suppliers.

The current separation of libraries and publishers will also have to be broken down, as Herman Spruijt described:

> "It looks to me as if what used to be a fight of tug-of-war between publishers and libraries is turning into more of a dance. We are twirling around each other, getting closer as the world is turning faster around us. We are still stepping on each other's toes, occasionally, as we are learning this new dance".

The word "partnership" has become widespread, but flags up another important aspect: the co-dependence of the various players in the market of digital information. New partnerships are necessary if users' expectations are to be met. Users are becoming increasingly more demanding, with the financial resources and human resources available to digital libraries being inadequate to satisfy their needs. There needs to be a transition from co-dependence to co-development. Win-win partnerships therefore have to be developed in order to overcome the obstacles presented by the current recession and to meet what are now the very different needs of the user.

VISION STATEMENT

At the end of the conference, the IFLA Professional Committee formulated a vision statement that will lead the way for the implementation of the digital libraries theme within the IFLA organisation over the next few years. This vision statement of digital library future is formulated as follows:

> To employ the potential of digital technology to its fullest extent in partnership with users by enabling seamless and open access to all types of information without limits with regard to format or geography. The methodology to be implemented to achieve this will be based on improving the ability of libraries, archives and museums to collaborate, not only with each other but also with third parties, in order to offer as full and as far reaching a service as possible.

This statement includes the main conclusions: a) technology is not enough, b) we need cooperation with users c) we need international cooperation with cultural institutions and d) we need to build new partnerships with others (publishers, et al.).

CLOSURE

Ellen Tise

After a full day with many interesting presentations and stimulating discussions, I have the honour to close this special conference day on digital library futures. The program organisers have managed to put together in a very short timeframe a varied international programme with a strong cross domain focus on digital library user perspectives and institutional strategies.

The user oriented approach of the digital library theme has strongly underlined the view of the IFLA Professional Committee that institutional strategies should take into account the different roles of the users in digital collections. The variety of presentations has stressed the importance to create and stimulate cooperation between libraries, museums, archives and publishers. Each of them has its own way of responding to the challenge of providing digital collections that meet the users' needs. But together they form a strong basis for an international digital network that helps to drive access to knowledge.

In the 2009–2011 period "Libraries driving access to knowledge" will be the leading theme for my two year presidential term. Convergence in the cultural heritage sector will remain a strong focus within IFLA through the international NGO's on Convergence Working Group, and of course, the cooperation between IFLA and IPA will be continued.

To be able to advocate for the library as driver for access to knowledge, libraries and librarians must include the perspective of the users in their operations.

To become in itself strong drivers for access to knowledge, libraries and librarians should create partnerships and foster opportunities for convergence with social stakeholders, commercial/private enterprises, cultural institutions and knowledge institutions. The digital library offers a strong asset to work on this.

I am happy to conclude that through its theme, this special conference day connects very well with my presidential theme and our current convergence initiatives in the LAMMS environment.

The goal of this conference was to stimulate a coherent working plan for IFLA and all its working groups in the area of digitisation. I consider the draft vision statement as formulated by Anna Maria Tammaro in the final summary to be a good basis for that. Digital Libraries could provide a strong connection between IFLA's Professional Programme and IFLA's Advocacy Programme. And I am fully confident that this day has been a good starting point for a sustainable follow up within IFLA. The first follow up will be tomorrow morning, when at the Plenary Session of the IFLA Congress this digital library futures conference and its outcome will be addressed.

I would like to thank both speakers and organisers for the efforts they have put into making this a successful conference day. I would like to thank all attendees for their active participation in this conference. I would like to thank the Athena Project Organisation and the University of Milano for their generous support, and last but not least I would like to thank the Italian Ministry of Culture for having taken the initiative for a conference on digital libraries at the event of our 75th World Library and Information Congress.

APPENDICES

BIOGRAPHIES

SESSION CHAIRS

Patrice Landry – Moderator
Patrice Landry has been Head of Subject Indexing at the Swiss National Library since 1996. He previously held different positions at the Library and Archives Canada. His main professional interests are in the field of subject headings languages, classification and multilingual subject access. He presently led the MACS project and is the current Chair of EDUG (European DDC Users' Group). In IFLA, he is the outgoing Chair of the Classification and Indexing section, as well as the outgoing Chair of the Bibliographic Control Section (Division IV). He is the newly elected Chair, IFLA Professional Committee (2009–2011). He is a member of the IFLA Governing Board and Executive Committee.

Caroline Brazier – Chair Session 1
Caroline Brazier is the Associate Director for Operations and Services at the British Library. Based at the Library's northern site at Boston Spa in Yorkshire, she is responsible for developing the service strategy and operational performance for the Library's Document Supply Service and also for contemporary collection acquisition and cataloguing. She is also responsible for the development of the services through which library users search, navigate, identify and access information resources through the Library's catalogues to meet their information needs. Before joining the British Library in 2002, Caroline had worked in a variety of professional library roles within the university and third level sector over a period of 20 years. Her key professional interests are in digital library technologies, library strategy development and customer service improvement. Caroline Brazier is chair of ICADS, the IFLA CDNL-Alliance for Digital Strategies.

Trine Kolderup-Flaten – Chair Session 2
Trine Kolderup-Flaten is Library Director of the Bergen Public Library since 1989. She started her career as Director of the County Library of Sogn og Fjordane, Norway (1965); was Editor of the University Press in Bergen, Norway from 1982–1985, Director of JW Eide publishing Company, Bergen (that she owned from 1989–2006). Trine has been a Member of Norwegian Cultural Council, member of advisory committees (1970–1982); Member of Advisory Committee for Nordic Cultural Ministers (1976–1980); Chair of the board, Norwegian School of Librarianship (1975–1980); Member of the board of Norwegian Distant Education; Member of the Norwegian Government's Advisory

Committee on Information Technology (1988–1991) and Chair of the International Edvard Grieg Society's Executive committee, member of the Executive committee since 1998. She served as Secretary of the IFLA Section on Management & Marketing from 2005–2009; Chair of the IFLA Division VI and Member of the IFLA Professional Committee and IFLA Governing Board from 2007–2009. This year Trine took up the role of Deputy chair of the Board for The Bergen International Opera.

Ingrid Parent – Chair Session 3
Ingrid Parent was recently appointed University Librarian at the University of British Columbia. From 1994 to 2004, she was Director General of Acquisitions and Bibliographic Services at the National Library of Canada, responsible for the development of the Library's collections, the organisation of information, and standards development. From 2004 to 2009, she was the Assistant Deputy Minister for the Documentary Heritage Collection Sector at Library and Archives Canada responsible for the development, the description and the preservation of the Canadian documentary heritage. She also co-led the development of the Canadian Digital Information Strategy. She was elected in 1999 to the Governing Board of the International Federation of Library Associations and Institutions (IFLA) and was also the IFLA Treasurer. She is the Chair of the IFLA Section on National Libraries and Co-chair of the joint IFLA/International Publishers Association steering committee. In June, 2009, IFLA elected her to serve as President-elect for the term 2009–2011 and to serve as President for the term 2011–2013. In May, 2009 the Canadian Association of Research Libraries (CARL) recognized Ms. Parent as the winner of the 2009 CARL award for Distinguished Service to Research Librarianship. Her related professional interests include international standards development, liaising with publishers on common interests, as well as working actively with other libraries and archives in matters related to organising, preserving and providing access to collections, including digital material.

Anna Maria Tammaro – Final Summary
Anna Maria Tammaro has been teaching "Digital Library" courses in Parma University, Italy since 1999 and she is the Italian Coordinator of the "Erasmus Mundus Master Digital Library Learning". She is the present Chair of the IFLA Division Education and Research and the Chair of the Section Education and Training. Her research interests are: Digital Library education, Internationalisation and quality of LIS education.

SPEAKERS – SESSION 1

David Nicholas

David Nicholas is Professor / Director of the Department of Information Studies at University College London. He is also the Director of the UCL Centre for Publishing and the CIBER research group. Previously, he was Head of Department of the Department of Information Science at the City University. His research interests largely concern mapping behaviour in virtual spaces, the virtual scholar, and the health information consumer.

Daniel Teruggi

Daniel Teruggi studied Physics, composition and piano in Argentina. In 1977 he came to France to study at the Paris Conservatory. In 1981, he began working at INA (National Audiovisual Institute), at the Groupe de Recherches Musicales (GRM). In 1997 he became Director of the Groupe de Recherches Musicales.

Since October 2001 he also directs the Research and Experimentation Department in INA. Teruggi has a PhD in Art and Technology in the Paris VIII University. He teaches Sound and Visual Arts, at the Paris I Sorbonne University. He is director of a Seminar on new technology applied to Musical analysis at the Paris IV University. He has developed an important activity as composer (more than 80 works) and researcher, mainly on the relations between creation and technology and on the problematic related to sound perception.

In recent years he has been actively working on the preservation of audiovisual collections and particularly the case of electro acoustic music, where traditional models of conservation are not effective. He has been the coordinator of the FP6 European project PrestoSpace. Actually coordinating the FP7 European project PrestoPRIME and participates in the Europeana project. He is a founding member of the Electro acoustic Musical Studies network (http://www.ems-network.org/), in charge of an annual conference on electro acoustic music analysis.

Elke Greifeneder

Elke Greifeneder is currently a lecturer at the Berlin School at Humboldt-Universität zu Berlin. She finished her master in Library and Information Science in 2007. Her thesis on online help systems in OPACs won the prize for the best master thesis in Austria, Switzerland and Germany. She is now working on her PhD on online user research. She studied both Library and Information Science and French studies in Berlin and Documentation and Linguistics in Paris. She has served as assistant editor of Library Hi Tech since 2006 and is a corresponding member of the IFLA Section on People with Special Needs since 2009.

SPEAKERS – SESSION 2

Einar Røttingen

Einar Røttingen is Professor of Music Performance and head of the Masters Program in Performance or Composition at the Grieg Academy, Department of Music, University of Bergen. He is also pianist and received his education at the Bergen Music Conservatory and Eastman School of Music. In addition to being a regular guest at the annual Bergen International Festival and Edvard Grieg Museum concert series in Norway, he has performed extensively as a soloist and chamber musician in major cities in Europe, USA and Asia. Throughout the 1980s, Røttingen worked closely with the Norwegian composer Harald Sæverud and has recorded all the solo piano music in addition to the Piano Concerto with Bergen Philharmonic Orchestra (Simax). He has also collaborated with many living composers and has commissioned numerous works. His recordings include the solo-CD *Avgarde* with works by Knut Vaage, Torstein Aagaard-Nilsen, Glenn Haugland, Jostein Stalheim and Ketil Hvoslef and others, *Hika* – with the violinist Trond Sæverud in works by Crumb, Takemitsu, Messiaen, Debussy and Grieg – and George Crumb's *Makrokosmos. Hika* was chosen as "Selection of the month" in *The Strad* in 2002. In 2005 Einar Røttingen was soloist with the Bergen Philharmonic Orchestra in the first performance of Knut Vaage's Piano Concerto *The Gardens of Hokkaido*. The solo-CD *Norwegian Variations*, which includes Grieg's *Ballade op.24* and *Sonatas* by Fartein Valen and Geirr Tveitt, was chosen as "Special Selection" in *International Piano* in 2006 and awarded "Record of the Year" by *The International Grieg Society of Great Britain*. This CD is also included in his PhD dissertation from 2006: *Establishing a Norwegian Piano Tradition: Interpretive Aspects of Edvard Grieg's Ballade op.24, Fartein Valen's Sonata no.2 op.38 and Geirr Tveitt's Sonata no.29 op.129*. In 2007 Røttingen performed the complete 172 songs of Edvard Grieg with the bass-baryton Njål Sparbo in a series of 7 concerts as part of the *Grieg September Festival* in Bergen. As a part of the 100th anniversary of Olivier Messiaen's birth in 2008 he performed, among other works, *Vingt Regards sur l'enfant Jesus* and *Des Canyons aux Etoiles*. Einar Røttingen has been awarded the *City of Bergen Cultural Prize* and The Bergen International Festival's *Robert Levin Festival Prize*.

Susan Hazan

Susan Hazan is Curator of New Media and Head of the Internet Office at the Israel Museum, Jerusalem (since 1992), identifying, and implementing electronic architectures for the gallery, and outreach programs (http://www.imj.org.il). Her Masters and PhD at Goldsmiths College, University of London in Media and Communications focused on electronic architectures in the contemporary museum. Hazan has been recognized for her numerous publications on new media in education, art, museums and cultural heritage, and is currently researching and publishing her research on Web 3.0 and persistent worlds. In 2002–2003 Hazan was visiting lecturer at the Computing Department at Gold-smiths, University of London; teaching Web Design and Critical E-Museology, with an emphasis on the correlation between cultural theory and contemporary practice. She is an annual guest lecturer in the Museology Department at Haifa University, Israel (2005–2009). Her professional affiliations include: EVA representative in Israel (http://www.evaconferences.com), World Summit Award (WSA) Israel Coordinator (http://www.wsis-award.org), founding partner in Digital Heritage, Israel (http://www.digital-heritage.org.il) and Co-Chair of the Annual Jerusalem Conference on the Digitisation of Cultural Heritage (http://www.minervaisrael.org.il). Hazan sits on the Museums and the Web – Program Committee 2001–2009, and for the Virtual Systems and MultiMedia Conferences to Europe (VSMM2005/2009), and on the Curatoral Panel for Netartsorg – Machida City Museum of Graphic Arts, Japan 2004–2009 (http://www.netarts.org). Hazan is consulting for both ATHENA (http://www.athenaeurope.org) and Europeana, Europeana v1.0 work package 1, work group 1.1: Users (http://www.europeana.eu/portal), as a specialist in Web 2.0 and social networks in the cultural sector. Hazan acts a Reviewer to Discovery Projects, Australian Research Council (ARC) and Independent Expert for EC Safer Internet Programme (http://ec.europa.eu/saferinternet).

SPEAKERS – SESSION 3

Zhu Qiang

Zhu Qiang is Professor and Director at the Peking University Library of the Peking University, Beijing 100871, China. He graduated from the Department of Library Science in Peking University, Zhu Qiang had worked in National Steering Committee for Academic Libraries for 8 years where he was a vice secretary-general since 1987. From 1990 to 1993, he was the assistant director and the head of Automation Division of the Peking University library. And then, he became the deputy director and director since 2008, and temporary the director of Shenzhen University Town Library from 2002 to 2005. He studied at the University of Illinois at Urbana-Champaign in 1994–1995 as a visiting scholar. He has also held the position of Chief Editor, *Journal of Academic Libraries* and Deputy Director, Administrative Center of China Academic Library & Information System (CALIS). He is also elected as the vice chairman of Library Society of China (2009–2013) and member of the Governing Board of IFLA (2009–2011). Mr. Zhu has published over 60 papers in the areas of academic library modernisation, library automation and resource-sharing system.

Rossella Caffo

Rossella Caffo is the director of the Central Institute for the Unified Catalogue of the Italian Libraries (ICCU) in Rome and is entrusted by the DG for the Technological Innovation and Promotion of the Italian Ministry for Cultural Heritage and Activities to follow ministerial initiatives dealing with new technologies applied to cultural heritage. In this capacity she coordinates national and international projects, such as the Italian Culture Portal, the European projects MINERVA, MinervaPLUS and MinervaEC, MICHAEL, MichaelPLUS and ATHENA. She directed the University library in Cagliari, the Information and Statistical Service of the General Secretary of the Italian Ministry for Culture from 2001 to 2004, and the Library of Modern and Contemporary History in Rome from 2005 to 2008. Since September 2001, Rossella Caffo was appointed by the Ministry for Cultural Heritage and Activities as Italian representative in the framework of the European National Representatives Group for digitisation of cultural heritage by the European Commission. This role has been renewed in April 2007 when she was officially appointed by the Italian Ministry as national representative in the Member States' Expert Group on Digitisation and Digital preservation, set up by the European Commission (Commission decision of 22 March 2007 – 2007/320 EC). Rossella Caffo was also responsible for the CREMISI project, which realised open distance learning training courses in the field of multimedia and IT devoted to librarians, and provided libraries with multimedia services and multimedia classrooms for training. Between 1994 and 1997 she was President of Italian Library Association (AIB) and from 1997 to 2001 was a member of the EBLIDA Executive Committee as the representative of Italian Library Association.

John Van Oudenaren

John Van Oudenaren directs the World Digital Library project at the Library of Congress. Previously he served as chief of the European Division at the Library and as the director of the Library's *Global Gateway* digital library projects. Prior to joining the Library in 1996, he was a senior researcher at the RAND Corporation in Santa Monica, California, and director of RAND's European office in Delft, the Netherlands. He has served on the Policy Planning Staff of the U.S. Department of State and has been a research associate at the International Institute for Strategic Studies in London. He received his Ph. D. in Political Science from the Massachusetts Institute of Technology and his A.B. in Germanic Languages and Literature from Princeton University. John Van Oudenaren has published several books and numerous articles on politics and international relations.

Herman P. Spruijt

Following studies in the University of Leiden, Herman P. Spruijt began his career at Kluwer Publishing Company in 1974, where he held a variety of positions in printing and publishing divisions. Between 1981 and 1987, he was a member of the board of directors of the newspaper group Perscombinatie, as statutory director and publisher responsible for *Trouw*, a Dutch national daily newspaper. In 1987 he entered Elsevier as Managing Director of the Physical Sciences and Engineering Division and after three years joined the board of directors. In 1994, he became Vice-Chairman and CEO and in 1995 he was appointed as Chairman of Elsevier Science and joined the board of Reed Elsevier PLC. Currently he is acting as Chairman of the Board of De Monchy and Royal BDU and board member of Royal Brill and the Financial Newspaper *Financieele Dagblad* in The Netherlands. After several years of associative work in the field of publishing, Herman P. Spruijt was elected President of the International Publishers Association (IPA) from 1 January 2009.

Penny Carnaby – Closing Address

Penny Carnaby is New Zealand's National Librarian and Chief Executive of the National Library of New Zealand, a position she has held since 2003. In 2007 the National Library announced an all-encompassing modernization programme: the New Generation National Library strategy will reshape and redefine services within an increasingly digital environment, build people capability to support new services, and improve infrastructure. In support of building a robust knowledge-based network for New Zealand, Penny has also led the National Library's digital strategy focused on digital content and the long-term preservation of New Zealand's digital assets. Penny Carnaby is Deputy Chair of the ICT Steering Committee for Education, a member of the Library and Information Advisory Commission (LIAC), and Adjunct Professor in the School of Information Management at Victoria University of Wellington. Penny is Chair of the Conference of Directors of National Libraries (CDNL), having been elected at the Seoul meeting in 2006. She is a member of National and State Libraries of Australasia (NSLA). Prior to taking up the leadership of the National Library of New Zealand, Penny was University Librarian at Macquarie University in Sydney, Australia. Previous to that, she enjoyed a long career in the tertiary sector in New Zealand, in several roles at Christchurch Polytechnic Institute of Technology (CPIT), including leading integrated education delivery services in library and learning services, e-learning and staff development. In 1999–2000 she served as National President of the Library and Information Association of New Zealand Aotearoa (LIANZA), and was awarded a Fellowship of the Association in 2001.

PHOTO IMPRESSIONS

The Venue

University of Milan

Registration

Audience (1)

Inauguration Session

Patrice Landry, Day Chair   Lux – Caffo – Franzini

Elio Franzini   Claudia Lux

First Session

Caroline Brazier, Chair

Nicolas – Teruggi – Greifeneder

David Nicholas

Daniel Teruggi

Elke Greifeneder

Second Session

Trine Kolderup-Flaten, Chair

Einar Røttingen

Susan Hazan

Third Session

Ingrid Parent, Chair

Parent and Zhu Qiang

Rossella Caffo

John Van Oudenaeren

Herman Spruijt

Closing Session

Penny Carnaby

AnnaMaria Tammaro

Patrice Landry and Ellen Tise

Audience (2)

Networking

Discussions

Aftermath